Pursuing
Purity

Virginia Lefler

Pursuing
Purity

Virginia Lefler

Silverday Press
185 Enfield Lane
Grayslake, IL 60030

For up-to-date information about
Silverday Press or to obtain more
information about this book, visit
www.SilverdayPress.com

Pursuing Purity

Published by Silverday Press — www.SilverdayPress.com

Printed in the United States of America.

Library of Congress Control Number: 2006906616

ISBN 10: 0-9729903-2-1
ISBN 13: 978-0-9729903-2-5

Cover Design: Pam Hamilton
                  www.pamhamdesign.com

Contents

To My Sisters in Christ,

It is my hope that this Bible study will stir up your thinking about purity and the many benefits that come from living a pure life. This is a very personal topic and it is not my intent to offend or embarrass. Rather, I hope to equip you with scriptures and strengthen your faith in God's plan for us to be pure.

1 Corinthians 2:7 says that God offers us a "secret wisdom," a wisdom that has been hidden from the world and that God destined for our glory before time began. In other words, God is giving us the inside scoop. God is setting us up for success. Purity is a much needed shield in our lives, a protection from evil. God isn't giving us a legalistic set of rules to obey; he is showing us the way to a glorious life. I pray that you hold onto these scriptures and fight the spiritual battle for a pure life. It's a battle worth fighting!

With love,

Virginia Lefler

– Chapter 1 –

God's Promises

As you read the following passage, focus on what God is promising you.

> *...As God has said: "I will live with them and walk among them, and I will be their God, and they will be my people."*
>
> *"Therefore come out from them and be separate, says the Lord. Touch no unclean thing, and I will receive you."*
>
> *"I will be a Father to you, and you will be my sons and daughters, says the Lord Almighty."*
>
> *Since we have these promises, dear friends, let us purify [katharizō] ourselves from everything that contaminates body and spirit, perfecting holiness out of reverence for God.*
>
> 2 Corinthians 6:16 - 7:1

Promises:
I will live with you.
I will walk with you.
I will receive you.
You will be my daughters.

God is offering himself to you in a loving, nurturing relationship – a Father/child relationship. The Lord Almighty wants to be your Father. How are we to respond to this incredible offer? Twice in this passage we are told to purify ourselves. The second time he says to purify ourselves from *everything* that contaminates body and spirit.

The Greek word translated "purify" is *katharizō*.

Definition: *Katharizō* (kath-ar-id´-zo); to cleanse (literal or figurative); make clean, purge, purify.[1]

The Bible has a lot to say about purity and offers us wisdom to fight this battle. This battle for purity is not easy even though we live in a "Christian" nation. In 2003, the Barna Group reported that 60% of our nation believes that cohabitation before marriage is morally acceptable, 40% believe adultery is morally acceptable, and 30% believe homosexuality is morally acceptable.[2]

Twenty years ago these statistics would not have been this high. Our moral standards are moving, but not in God's direction. This can make the battle for purity even more challenging, but it also makes it more important than ever to be aware of it. As the moral standards slip, we need to be all the more engaged in this spiritual battle.

We need to know that God is with us, and we also need to know our enemy and the schemes he uses against us. 1 Peter 5:8 says our enemy is like a hungry, roaring lion who wants to devour us. Ephesians 6:12 says our battle is against the powers of this dark world and against the spiritual forces of evil in the heavenly realms.

* * *

How pure do I need to be? What is the goal? Consider the following scripture:

> *Dear friends, now we are children of God, and what we will be has not yet been made known. But we know that when he appears, we shall be like him, for we shall see him as he is. Everyone who has this hope in him purifies [hagnizo] himself, just as he is pure [hagnos].*
>
> 1 John 3:2-3

Promises:
We shall be like him.
We shall see him.

Definition: *Hagnizo* (hag-nid-zo); to make clean, i.e. (figurative) sanctify (ceremony or moral); purify (self).[3]

Definition: *Hagnos* (hag-nos´); innocent, modest, perfect – chaste, clean, pure.[4]

This verse says that God is our standard. This standard will keep us busy for the rest of our lives. Of course, being in Christ is the only way that we can measure up. Consider the following scripture:

But if we walk in the light, as he is in the light, we have fellowship with one another, and the blood of Jesus, his Son, <u>purifies us</u> from all sin. [Emphasis added.]

1 John 1:7

Jesus' blood continues to purify us. There are two responses that we might have to this wonderful mercy and forgiveness. One, you might be tempted to take advantage of it. The following verse addresses this response:

What shall we say, then? Shall we go on sinning so that grace may increase? By no means! We died to sin; how can we live in it any longer?

Romans 6:1-2

The other response is appreciation and devotion.

So then, dear friends, since you are looking forward to this, make every effort to be found spotless, blameless and at peace with him.

2 Peter 3:14

For you were once darkness, but now you are light in the Lord. Live as children of light (for the fruit of the light consists in all goodness, righteousness and truth) and find out what pleases the Lord. Have nothing to do with the fruitless deeds of darkness, but rather expose them.

Ephesians 5:8-11

These scriptures encourage us to respond aggressively to God's love and mercy by:

- making every effort,
- finding out what pleases the Lord, and
- having nothing to do with deeds of darkness.

Every day we make choices that impact our purity before God. We need to be alert and strong. A myth we face today is that a worldly woman is a strong woman, and a pure woman is naive and vulnerable. Nothing could be further from the truth. It takes a strong person to live a pure life. And I'm not referring to someone who has been isolated from the world and never had an opportunity to experience a lot of sin. I'm talking about making choices and drawing close to God by the way we live. It takes spiritual strength to turn off the television or leave the theater when you find yourself watching something you should not. It takes strength to make choices that go against the worldly standards we see all around us. It's a battle we have to fight every day.

A better description of a worldly woman is hardened, rather than strong. There is a hardening process that goes on in our hearts when we sin (Hebrews 3:7-13). And the more one sins, the harder the heart. A hard heart does not make us strong. Becoming pure like God is how we gain strength. It is the opposite of what the world thinks.

As a young Christian, I remember trying to change some things in my life and realizing that it was not going to be easy. My spiritual muscles were very weak, and I needed to strengthen them. Hardening my heart was not the solution.

Striving for purity is a lifelong process. This isn't a battle just for young people. We even see people in the Bible who struggled with impurity in their later years (David, Noah, Lot).

If you are young, I encourage you to put your whole heart into striving for purity. It won't be easier when you get older or married. If you put off becoming pure, you will miss many blessings in your life. Impurity has a big price tag on it. Abraham's nephew Lot is an example of someone who tried to have both God and the world, and his life was a disaster.

There are many things we face daily that are an assault on the very heart of our purity. We are bombarded with advertisers trying to get us to buy their products, go to their movies and watch their TV shows. Television shows like *Desperate Housewives* and *Sex In The City* flaunt impurity and immorality. Even the advertisements for these shows have caused controversy when shown during family hours. And the business world is certainly no haven from the battle for purity.

We might call our own battle "Desperate Christian Women," except that we have a secret weapon when it comes to fighting this battle -- the Holy Spirit. Consider the following verses about the Holy Spirit:

Peter replied, "Repent and be baptized, every one of you, in the name of Jesus Christ for the forgiveness of your sins. And you will receive the gift of the Holy Spirit." [Emphasis added.]

Acts 2:38

But the fruit of the Spirit is love, joy, peace, patience, kindness, goodness, faithfulness, gentleness and self-control. Against such things there is no law. Those who belong to Christ Jesus have crucified the sinful nature with its passions and desires. Since we live by the Spirit, let us keep in step with the Spirit. [Emphasis added.]

Galatians 5:22-25

For God did not give us a spirit of timidity, but a spirit of power, of love and of self-discipline. [Emphasis added.]

2 Timothy 1:7

We often honor someone after a baptism with little gifts to commemorate the occasion. But God goes all out to commemorate this special event. He gives them the gift of the Holy Spirit (Acts 2:38). Wow! You will receive no greater gift in all of your lifetime! The Holy Spirit will strengthen you (Ephesians 3:16), guide you (John 16:13) and help you overcome sin (Romans 8:13).

I want to encourage you as you go through this study to let the Holy Spirit guide you. The fruit of the Holy Spirit (love, joy, peace, self-control, etc.) is sought after by many people, but God grants these qualities through his Spirit. Pray that God will help you be aware of his Holy Spirit and that you keep in step with him as you go through this study. He will guide you in the ways he wants you to go.

Worksheet 1 - God's Promises

Consider again 1 John 3:2-3. Are you zealous for purity in your life? In what ways do God's promises regarding purity impact you?

How do you perceive someone who is pure? Do you equate purity with naivety and vulnerability or with strength and honor?

Meditation: Read 2 Corinthians 6:16 - 7:1. Consider God's greatness as you go through this day and remember his desire to be your Father. Consider also your response to this amazing offer and ways you can grow in your purity.

Memory Verse: 2 Corinthians 7:1

– Chapter 2 –

Spiritual Beauty

Your beauty should not come from outward adornment, such as braided hair and the wearing of gold jewelry and fine clothes. Instead, it should be that of your inner self, the unfading beauty of a gentle and quiet spirit, which is of great worth in God's sight. For this is the way the holy women of the past who put their hope in God used to make themselves beautiful...
1 Peter 3:3-5

Before we begin to consider how to grow in purity, I first want to discuss spiritual beauty. Spiritual beauty and purity are closely connected, and understanding spiritual beauty will help build a foundation for growing in purity.

The above scripture tells us that we can be beautiful to God. However, this beauty is not like physical beauty. We gain this beauty by our spiritual choices.

There is a natural desire in us to be beautiful and to have beautiful things. It's important to remember that God created beauty and that our love for beautiful things is God-given. He did not create the world in black and white. He created a marvelous world that can take our breath away. Beauty is a basic human pleasure given by God.

A recent study commissioned by Dove, a Unilever Beauty Brand company, titled, *The Real Truth about Beauty: A Global Report,* found that only 2% of the women whom they surveyed would describe themselves as beautiful. The study also stated that "beauty" is not only a word that women are very unlikely to choose to describe their looks; it is also one which many actually feel uncomfortable using to describe themselves. The top two descriptors were "average" and "natural."[5]

The media has had a huge impact on how we view our own beauty. According to the Dove study, we see about 2,000 images each week on what or who the media defines as beautiful.[6] Webster's defines beauty as the quality attributed to whatever pleases or satisfies the senses or mind, as by line, color, form, texture, proportion, rhythmic motion, tone, etc., or by behavior or attitude.[7] This is a much broader definition than what we see in the media. The narrow media definition has influenced us in many ways. Even some of the most beautiful women do not feel beautiful.

The relationship that we have with beauty is complex: it can be powerful and inspiring, but elusive and frustrating, as well.[8] How do you feel about the topic of beauty? Do you feel beautiful? Hopefully, you do. But if you don't, I have great news! Spiritual beauty is for absolutely every one of us. And we don't want to think "average" when it comes to our spiritual beauty. This is a beauty in which every one of us can excel.

There are two questions I want to briefly answer concerning spiritual beauty: What is it and why would I want it?

What is it?

Unlike physical beauty, spiritual beauty is not something you are born with or without. And you cannot go to a surgeon to get any spiritual enhancements. This is a beauty that must be developed. It is an equal-opportunity beauty, because no one can keep you from it except you. Consider 1 Peter 3:3-5 again in the New American Standard Version:

> *Your adornment must not be merely external—braiding the hair, and wearing gold jewelry, or putting on dresses; but let it be the hidden person of the heart, with the imperishable quality of a gentle and quiet spirit, which is precious in the sight of God. For in this way in former times the holy women also, who hoped in God, used to adorn themselves...*
>
> 1 Peter 3:3-5 (NASB)

14

This passage gives us several insights into spiritual beauty. First, spiritual beauty involves the hidden person of the heart. For spiritual beauty, you cannot go through a checklist: moisturizer – check; foundation – check; blush – check; eye shadow – check; mascara – check. You get the idea. We cannot do that in a spiritual way. Beautifying our hearts takes consideration and transformation from the inside out.

Another characteristic of spiritual beauty is that it's imperishable. The only thing you get to take with you from this world is your soul. You need to make it a priority to develop your spiritual beauty. You will take this beauty into heaven.

This passage also tells us that a gentle and quiet spirit is an important aspect of being spiritually beautiful. These qualities are perceived by many women as weak or passive qualities. However, the truth is that the original Greek text describes a strong and peaceful woman. The following excerpt from my book, *A Gentle & Quiet Spirit,* explains these qualities:

Gentle

The Greek word translated "gentle" or "meek" is *praus*.

Definition: *Praus* (prah-ooce´); the exercises of it are first toward God. It is that temper of spirit in which we accept his dealings with us as good without disputing or resisting and is closely linked with the word humility. It is only the humble heart which is also *praus*, and which, as such, does not fight against God. *Praus* is the opposite of self-assertiveness and self-interest.

The meaning of *praus* is not readily expressed in English, for the terms gentleness and meekness, commonly used, suggest weakness, whereas *praus* does nothing of the kind. The common assumption is that when a man is meek or gentle, it is because he cannot help himself, but the Lord was *praus* because he had the infinite resources of God at his command.[9]

Praus means power under control, or power that is submitted or surrendered. It takes great inner strength to be

15

praus. The English word gentleness refers more to actions, whereas *praus* refers more to a condition of mind and heart.[10] Our modern usage for "gentle" and "meek" is being mild or weak, lacking in spirit and courage. Having no inner strength and being easily imposed upon is how some people perceive a gentle and quiet spirit. Maybe that's the way Pilate viewed Jesus in Matthew 27:13-14, but Jesus was not replying *because* he had inner strength. Consider Jesus in the following verse. Imagine this taking place.

> Say to the Daughter of Zion, "See, your king comes to you, gentle [praus] and riding on a donkey, on a colt, the foal of a donkey."
>
> Matthew 21:5

Do you picture Jesus looking docile as he rode a donkey into Jerusalem? Read the definition of *praus* again and think about Jesus entering Jerusalem. When it says Jesus was *praus*, it's describing his attitude toward God. Jesus knew he was facing crucifixion, yet he was willing to go into Jerusalem. He was *praus.*

When Jesus was arrested, he said in Matthew 26:53, *"Do you think I cannot call on my Father, and he will at once put at my disposal more than twelve legions of angels?"* A legion is an army of up to 5,000 men.[11] So Jesus is saying that he could have immediately called more than 60,000 angels. One would have been enough! He had this infinite power that we cannot fathom. Consider this for a moment. Jesus was gentle (*praus*) because he had incredible power at his disposal and he chose not to use it. Instead he submitted himself to God and made himself available for God's plan for his life.

When I studied the Greek word *praus* and found that it described a strong woman instead of a weak one, it drastically changed how I read this verse. I found it more appealing.

Quiet

The Greek word translated "quiet" is *hesuchios*.

> **Definition**: *Hesuchios* (hay-soo´-khee-os); tranquillity aris-
> ing from within,[12] undisturbed and undisturbing, peace-
> able, and quiet.[13]

As a young child, I lived near a spring of water where
my father would fill our water cans. Someone had put a
concrete liner in the ground around the spring so that it
was easy to draw the water out. I loved to go there. It was
a peaceful place where water constantly bubbled up from
within the earth and overflowed. It was puzzling to me
how year after year the water kept coming. There was an
invisible underground source that I could not understand
as a child. I think of that spring every time I read this
definition of "tranquillity arising from within." The quiet
spirit also has an unseen source. It comes from a deep
trust in God's love, protection and promises.

There are a lot of things we face every day that reveal
whether or not we have this kind of spirit. Does "tranquillity arising from within" describe you or would the
words "stressed-out" be a better fit? Stress, not tranquillity, describes many women today. Think back on what the
last week was like for you and your household. Were you
undisturbed by the events you faced and undisturbing to
others around you? Did you raise your voice or somehow
lose control? Were you peaceful in the middle of all your
busyness? Now, I assume you have been busy. We aren't
talking about whether or not you have a life of leisure, we
are talking about an inner quality.

Again, Jesus is the perfect example of *hesuchios*. Large
crowds of people who were needy, hungry and sick often surrounded him (sounds like a family at times). Luke
8:42 says, "As Jesus was on his way, the crowds almost
crushed him." It goes on to say that a woman touched him

17

and that Jesus took the time to inquire about it. Unlike his disciples, who urged Jesus to send needy people away (Mark 6:36), Jesus was unruffled by the crowds. We also read about him sleeping in a boat during a storm. You can see his incredible peace and his trust in God as he deals with his disciples' fear (Matthew 8:23-26).

Jesus completely trusted God. Consider the following passage:

> *For I did not speak of my own accord, but the Father who sent me commanded me what to say and how to say it. I know that his command leads to eternal life. So whatever I say is just what the Father has told me to say.*
>
> John 12:49-50

He knew that God's commands would lead him to eternal life, in other words, get him back to heaven. He trusted God completely, including what to say and how to say it. What a remarkable level of trust!

There are many scriptures that give us direction on what to say and not say and how to say it and not say it. It's my goal to trust God completely, but occasionally my level of tranquillity shows me that I don't. When I'm in a stressful situation is when I'm most apt to say and do things that I later regret. At these times, I can usually find that I'm not trusting God about something. Consider the following scriptures:

> *May the God of hope fill you with all joy and peace as you trust in him, so that you may overflow with hope by the power of the Holy Spirit.*
>
> Romans 15:13

> *Trust in him at all times, O people; pour out your hearts to him, for God is our refuge.*
>
> Psalms 62:8

> *Do not let your hearts be troubled. Trust in God; trust also in me.*
>
> John 14:1

The quiet spirit is not a "fluff" quality. It comes from a deep trust in God's love, protection and promises.

A woman with a gentle and quiet spirit is an amazing woman. She is a woman with great inner strength, who has a close relationship with God. She trusts God to direct her, and she is overflowing with peace. She is both *praus* and *hesuchios*.[14]

Can you imagine how God must feel about this woman with a gentle and quiet spirit? She trusts him completely and she is surrendered to his will. She is spiritually beautiful!

Following are a few more scriptures that give insight into spiritual qualities and spiritual garments available to us:

> *...for all of you who were baptized into Christ have clothed yourselves with Christ.*
>
> Galatians 3:27

The most important spiritual garment we can clothe ourselves with is Christ. This happened at your baptism. 2 Corinthians 5:3 says that when we are clothed, we will not be found naked. We went from being spiritually naked to spiritually clothed in a beautiful way. And your blemishes (sins) are not just covered with a little makeup, they are actually gone (Colossians 1:22).

* * *

> *She is clothed with strength and dignity; she can laugh at the days to come.*
>
> Proverbs 31:25

Would you like to wear strength and dignity? Both of these qualities give us confidence. Maybe that is why "she can laugh at the days to come." In the Dove study, 86% percent of the women surveyed agreed that not only is happiness the primary element making a woman beautiful, but they strongly agreed that they themselves feel most beautiful when they are happy and fulfilled in their lives.[15]

* * *

Awake, awake, O Zion, clothe yourself with strength. Put on your garments of splendor, O Jerusalem, the holy city...

Isaiah 52:1

This is another reference to strength. It also mentions garments of splendor. Spiritually you can be dressed up.

* * *

...bestow on them a crown of beauty instead of ashes, the oil of gladness instead of mourning, and a garment of praise instead of a spirit of despair...

Isaiah 61:3

This verse gives a striking contrast. Do you want to wear a beautiful crown or ashes on your head? Do you want to be happy or sad? Do you want to be filled with praise or despair? These are easy questions to answer!

* * *

For this is the way the holy women of the past who put their hope in God used to make themselves beautiful. They were submissive to their own husbands,

1 Peter 3:5

Submission is also an adorning quality. This is how "holy" women make themselves beautiful.

* * *

Therefore, as God's chosen people, holy and dearly loved, clothe yourselves with compassion, kindness, humility, gentleness and patience.

Colossians 3:12

Kindness, compassion, humility, gentleness and patience are qualities of spiritual beauty. Tabitha was known for abounding with deeds of "kindness and charity" (Acts 9:36 NASB). We are not told what she looked like, but we know her spirit was clothed beautifully.

* * *

Summing up spiritual beauty is not easy because beauty has many facets. Spiritual beauty is first and foremost about our relationship with

God, whether or not we trust him and are surrendered to him (a gentle and quiet spirit). Other facets of spiritual beauty are compassion, kindness, self-control, humility, courage, love, happiness, patience, contentment, faithfulness, peace, etc.

Why would I want it?

Besides the appeal of these qualities, the most important reason to develop these qualities is that they are of great worth to God.

> *Instead, it should be that of your inner self, the unfading beauty of a gentle and quiet spirit, <u>which is of great worth in God's sight</u>.* [Emphasis added.]
>
> 1 Peter 3:4

The following is another excerpt from *A Gentle & Quiet Spirit* which explains how much God values this inner beauty:

Great Worth

Can you imagine something being valuable to God? He is the creator. Doesn't he have everything? We read in the Bible that he doesn't need anything (Acts 17:25); however, 1 Peter 3:4 says that there is something that is of great worth to him.

The Greek word translated "great worth" is *poluteles*.

Definition: *Poluteles* (pol-oo-tel-ace); the very end or limit with reference to price; of the highest cost, very expensive, very precious.[16]

Poluteles means the *very* end or limit. In other words, this is at the top of God's list of what he considers most precious to him.

What do you think God values? Is a gentle and quiet spirit something that you would have listed as one of the things that is highly valued by God?

What do you value the most? I have a diamond engagement ring that I cherish. I treat it with great care because of its value and its sentimental significance. I have many other things I value and protect, but they are not at the top of my list. My family tops my list. I would give up my life for them. They are priceless to me.

Sometimes it's not clear what we mean by the word great. If you are single and I set you up on a blind date and told you that this guy is great, you might ask me some questions. "What's great about him?" Or, "How great is 'great'?"

We often use the word great in a casual way. We might say that it's a great day, but we are only casually comparing the last few days. However, God is not saying "great" casually. *Poluteles* means the very end or limit with reference to value. This Greek word is also used in Mark 14:3-5.

> *... a woman came with an alabaster jar of very expensive [poluteles] perfume, made of pure nard. She broke the jar and poured the perfume on his head...It could have been sold for more than a year's wages...*
>
> Mark 14:3-5

This passage gives us more insight into the word *poluteles*. This perfume was worth more than a year's salary. Personally, I've never spent more than half of what I make in one day for perfume. Most perfumes today cost between $25 and $100. The most expensive perfume that I've ever seen cost $400 an ounce. But even that perfume would not be close in comparison to a perfume that cost more than a year's salary.

If you had a bottle of perfume that cost more than what you make in a year (or could make), how would you take care of it compared to your other perfumes? And how would you describe it compared to your other perfumes? I probably would repeat the word "very" several times just so that it is clear how valuable it is – "very, very, very expensive perfume." When you compare this perfume that was poured on Jesus with any other perfume, it is by far the most valuable.

When God says *poluteles* in 1 Peter 3:4, he means GREAT worth or VERY precious. This tops his list. A gentle and quiet spirit is of incredible worth to him.[17]

It can be difficult to accept that God values these qualities this much, especially if you have misunderstood them and have not placed a high value on them yourself. But the truth is God greatly values these qualities. They are of great worth to him!

Besides the appeal of these qualities and the value God places on them, spiritual beauty is also powerful. Physical beauty is powerful in that it can turn a man's head. According to the Dove study, 45% of all women strongly agree that "women who are more beautiful have greater opportunities in life."[18] Spiritual beauty is powerful for another reason. It is powerful because God is with you.

> *The LORD your God is with you, he is mighty to save. He will take great delight in you, he will quiet you with his love, he will rejoice over you with singing."*
>
> Zephaniah 3:17

A woman with spiritual beauty has a powerful life. She is clothed with strength, and she walks with God.

Worksheet 2 - Spiritual Beauty

How would you describe a spiritually beautiful woman?

Do you trust God and are you surrendered to him?

Which qualities of spiritual beauty are your strength?

Which qualities would you like to add to your own spiritual beauty?

Memory Verse: Proverbs 31:30-31

– Chapter 3 –

Spiritual Adornment

For in this way in former times the holy women also, who hoped in God, used to adorn themselves…

1 Peter 3:5 (NASB)

Spiritual beauty is amazing and I want it! So how do I become spiritually beautiful? When I want to improve my physical beauty, I first go stand in front of a mirror and evaluate myself. This is also true for spiritual beauty. We need to look into the spiritual mirror. The following verse describes the Bible as a mirror:

Do not merely listen to the word, and so deceive yourselves. Do what it says. Anyone who listens to the word but does not do what it says is like a man who looks at his face in a mirror and, after looking at himself, goes away and immediately forgets what he looks like. But the man who looks intently into the perfect law that gives freedom, and continues to do this, not forgetting what he has heard, but doing it--he will be blessed in what he does.

James 1:22-25

Promise:
You will be blessed.

We have been given a spiritual mirror, and we need to look into it intently. That mirror is the Bible. The Bible is a powerful mirror. Hebrews 4:12 says that God's word judges the thoughts and attitudes of the heart. It can reflect back to us our deepest thoughts and attitudes, and it will help us judge whether they are good or bad. It can reveal to us things that will change us forever.

How blessed we are to live during a time when Bibles are so available to us. If you need to purchase a Bible, you can go to almost any store that sells books and find a selection of Bibles. The most difficult part of this purchase is deciding what color, size and whether you want bonded or genuine leather. But this has not always been the case. Not too many centuries ago purchasing a Bible was a dangerous activity.

For many centuries, the Roman Catholic Church and the world leaders under its domain kept the scriptures from common people. In fact, they threatened anyone possessing a non-Latin Bible with execution.

In the 1380's John Wycliffe, an Oxford professor, produced the first hand-written English language Bible manuscripts. With the help of faithful scribes, he produced dozens of English language manuscripts of the Bible. The Pope was so infuriated by his teachings and his translation of the Bible into English, that 44 years after Wycliffe had died, he ordered Wycliffe's bones to be dug up, crushed and scattered in the river!

In the 1490's Thomas Linacre, another Oxford professor and the personal physician to King Henry VII and King Henry VIII, decided to learn Greek. After reading the Gospels in Greek, and comparing it to the Latin Vulgate, he wrote in his diary, "Either this (the original Greek) is not the Gospel... or we are not Christians." The Latin had become so corrupt that it no longer even preserved the message of the Gospel... yet the Church still threatened to kill anyone who read the scripture in any language other than Latin.

It was a turbulent time for the reformers. According to Foxe's Book of Martyrs, in 1517, seven people were burned at the stake by the Roman Catholic Church for the crime of teaching their children the Lord's prayer in English rather than Latin.

The printing press was invented in the 1450's, and the first book to ever be printed was a Latin language Bible. By the early 1500's, Martin Luther and William Tyndale were printing New Testaments they had translated into German and English, respectively, from the original Greek text.

Tyndale's copies of the New Testament made their way into England despite the efforts of King Henry VIII to confiscate them. Tyndale was eventually burned at the stake in 1536. Ironically, three years later, King Henry VIII allowed, and even funded, the printing of the English Bible in defiance of the Pope. The King had asked the Pope to grant him a divorce so that he could marry his mistress. When the Pope refused, the King responded by separating himself from the Catholic Church and starting the Anglican Church or the Church of England.

However this battle was still not over. Later when Queen "Bloody" Mary took the throne, she wanted to reunite with the Catholic Church and again made it illegal to own a non-Latin Bible.[19]

The following story is about a young woman who lived during this turbulent time:

Wrunken was a young maid who lived in Roneses, Flanders in the 1500's. She worked for the Mayor of Brugge. Philip II sent the Duke of Alba to Flanders to stamp out the Protestants who insisted on reading the Scriptures in their own language. Anyone found studying the Bible was hanged, drowned, torn in pieces or burned alive at the stake.

As they searched the mayor's home, a bible was discovered. One by one, family members were questioned, but everyone claimed they knew nothing about how the Bible got into their house. Finally, the officials asked the young maid-servant, Wrunken, who boldly declared, "I am reading it."

The mayor, knowing the penalty for studying the Bible, tried to defend her, saying, "Oh, no she only owns it. She doesn't ever read from it."

But Wrunken chose not to be defended by a lie. "This book is mine. I am reading from it, and it is more precious to me than anything."

She was sentenced to die by suffocation. A place would be hollowed in the city wall, she would be tied in it, and the opening would be bricked over.

On the day of her execution, as she stood by the wall, an official tried to get her to change her mind, saying, "So young and beautiful – and yet to die."

Wrunken replied, "My Savior died for me. I will also die for Him."

As the bricks were laid higher and higher, she was warned again. "You will suffocate and die in here."

"I will be with Jesus," she answered.

Finally, the wall was finished, except for the one brick that would cover her face. For the last time, the official tried to persuade her. "Repent – just say the word and you will go free."

But Wrunken refused, saying instead, "O Lord, forgive my murderers."

The brick was put in place. Many years later, her bones were removed from the wall and buried in the cemetery of Brugge.[20]

* * *

During this period in history, many people gave their lives for the privilege of reading the Bible. Today we do not fear being put to death for reading the Bible, but Satan still has many schemes to keep us from God's word. The following story illustrates one of them:

> *As Jesus and his disciples were on their way, he came to a village where a woman named Martha opened her home to him. She had a sister called Mary, who sat at the Lord's feet listening to what he said. But Martha was distracted by all the preparations that had to be made. She came to him and asked, "Lord, don't you care that my sister has left me to do the work by myself? Tell her to help me!"*
>
> *"Martha, Martha," the Lord answered, "you are worried and upset about many things, but only one thing is needed. Mary*

has chosen what is better, and it will not be taken away from her."

Luke 10:38-42

In this story we see how the pressures of Martha's life pulled her away from her time with Jesus. This is just one of the many schemes Satan uses to keep us from reading and studying God's word.

We also see the impact of Martha's choice. She is upset with Mary for not helping her and with Jesus for not caring. Her own spiritual condition was not obvious to her. She needed Jesus to help her see the truth about herself.

The Christians mentioned in the following scripture also had a distorted view of their true spiritual condition:

Revelation 3:17 You say, "I am rich; I have acquired wealth and do not need a thing." But you do not realize that you are wretched, pitiful, poor, blind and naked.

Revelation 3:17

It must have been quite a shock to hear these words. I would not want to be described by any one of them -- wretched, pitiful, poor, blind or naked! This is another example of why we need our spiritual mirror to reflect back to us so we can see how to become spiritually beautiful.

Many years ago when my sons were preschoolers, I baby-sat for three women in my neighborhood. One morning I overslept and had to rush to get ready for their arrival. I quickly glanced into my bathroom mirror as I headed to the kitchen to start cooking breakfast. I shocked myself by what I saw. The night before, I had been over-zealous in my use of an acne product for my face. I had dried spots all over my face. I intended to return and clean my face, but I forgot. It was just like James 1:24 says, "after looking at himself, goes away and *immediately* forgets what he looks like."

The three women, looking very professional, dropped off their children. A few minutes after the last one dropped off her child, I happened to walk by the mirror again. I was so embarrassed!

29

We can feel the same way about our spiritual flaws. Mirrors can show us some things we would rather not see. However, it would not have helped me to not look into the mirror again. I still had the spots on my face. Don't let the truth in the scriptures keep you from looking into this amazing spiritual mirror. It can help you make changes. And remember that James 1:25 says we will be blessed by looking intently into God's law if we will put it into practice.

Another thing to consider about a mirror is that it's a time of self-reflection. It's not a time to consider how someone else looks, but a time to consider your own reflection. I don't get up in the morning, go stand before my bathroom mirror and think, "I've seen *so-and-so's* hair look a lot worse than mine!" No, I think, "My hair is a mess! I've got to wash it." I'm there to evaluate my own issues. When I'm reading my Bible in the morning, it's a time to let the scriptures reflect back to me things I need to see about myself and ways I can make myself more beautiful to God.

This is important to consider, especially if you study the Bible to prepare lessons that you will teach, or if you study the Bible with other women helping them understand the scriptures. This should not be the extent of your personal study. That would be like a beautician who never styles her own hair while she helps other women look more beautiful. We need to come before our spiritual mirror every day to evaluate our own heart before God. What a shame it would be to help other women be beautiful before God but not personally enjoy spiritual beauty each day.

Another analogy about mirrors I would like you to consider is the use of a second mirror. When I want to check the back of my hair, I take my small hand mirror, turn around and look into the small mirror so I can see the back of my hair in my big mirror. Or when I'm trying on a new outfit at a dress shop, I will stand in front of a three-way mirror so I can see how this outfit looks all the way around. A second or third mirror helps me get a perspective that one mirror can't give me. As much as I try, I cannot get a complete picture by using only one mirror.

The same is true of my spiritual mirror. That second mirror is like the discipleship of an honest Christian sister who will help me see things in my life that I don't see. I need discipleship to help me see a more complete view of myself. I appreciate the many sisters who have helped me understand the scriptures, and I've benefited in many ways from their perspective.

Discipleship is important to your spiritual growth. It will give you a much needed second perspective in your life. However discipleship without your own deep Bible study is not a healthy balance either. If you expect someone else to teach you everything, you will miss many blessings.

> *Do your best to present yourself to God as one approved, a workman who does not need to be ashamed and who correctly handles the word of truth.*
>
> 2 Timothy 2:15

We must look intently into God's word. It will strengthen us and bring us closer to God. It will guide us as we consider how to grow in our spiritual beauty and how to fight the battle for more purity. Keep your spiritual mirror close by and look into it often.

* * *

Looking into the spiritual mirror is only the beginning. The next step is to take action. We must begin to adorn ourselves spiritually. The following scripture tells us that good deeds are part of our spiritual adornment:

> *I also want women to dress modestly, with decency and propriety, not with braided hair or gold or pearls or expensive clothes, but with good deeds, appropriate for women who profess to worship God.*
>
> 1 Timothy 2:9-10

This scripture gives us insight into spiritual adornment, but it also raises a question. Does this scripture mean we can't wear gold, pearls, braided hair or expensive clothing? If we take this scripture literally, we are told to wear good deeds. How modest would that be? This verse is not meant to create a dress code. We know as Christians that we have many freedoms in Christ. Not wearing gold or not braiding your hair will not necessarily make you a more godly woman. However, there are some important guidelines about modesty and decency in this verse. And there is also a very important principle of true beauty we must understand: **Your godly actions are more adorning than beautiful jewelry or expensive clothing**.

1 Peter 3:3-5 also makes a similar comparison of physical adornment to spiritual qualities:

> *Your adornment must not be merely external—braiding the hair, and wearing gold jewelry, or putting on dresses; but let it be the hidden person of the heart, with the imperishable quality of a gentle and quiet spirit, which is precious in the sight of God. For in this way in former times the holy women also, who hoped in God, used to adorn themselves...*
>
> 1 Peter 3:3-5 (NASB)

Some of the most beautiful things we can wear are gold and jewels. Do these things really make us more beautiful? I believe most women would answer yes to that question. Personally, I like a little sparkle on my ears! I think that it spiffs me up a little.

The point of these scriptures is that godliness is by far more beautifying than these lovely things with which we can adorn ourselves. We know how to improve our physical beauty, and we go to great lengths and expense to do so. But as women who profess to worship God, our beauty must go much deeper than what we adorn ourselves with on the outside. We must also adorn ourselves with spiritual qualities. In the long run, it is our spiritual beauty that really matters.

Spiritual beauty has many benefits. Did you know that our spiritual beauty actually spills over into our physical beauty? Conduct a test the next time you get dressed up. After you have done everything to look your very best, stand in front of a mirror and put anger on your face. How does that make you look? Then put happiness on your face. Or try putting fear or worry on your face, then melt it away with trusting thoughts about God. Isn't that the quickest beauty treatment you have ever seen? (I'm serious. Do this. It may seem a little crazy, but it will give you deeper convictions about inner beauty.)

I've seen women grow in their beauty when they became Christians. Faithful Christian women are some of the most beautiful women I know. They overcame fear, anger, worry, hatred, etc., by their faith in God. There is an inner beauty that shows through -- a beauty that no spa treatment can bring about. It's a beauty that comes from a faithful and contented life.

Our early Christian sisters took 1 Timothy 2:9-10 to heart. Tertullian (155-230 A.D.), a church leader and author, wrote about the spiritual wealth and worthiness of Christian women and how their modesty and simplicity was a rebuke to the shameless extravagancies of the heathen women.[21]

Libanius (314-394 A.D.), a pagan who was an educated, Greek-speaking teacher, is said to have exclaimed in admiration and astonishment, "What women these Christians have!"[22] I wonder why Libanius was so impressed by our early Christian sisters? Was he impressed by their willingness to die for Jesus or their submission to their husbands? Perhaps it was their purity, happiness or contentment. We aren't told why Libanius was impressed, but just that he was amazed by them.

What do you think impresses a man? Is he more impressed by jewelry or actions? Personally, I don't think it's our jewelry. Women are much more interested in jewelry than most men. My husband is more impressed by my happiness than if I wore a beautiful piece of jewelry. He loves it when I'm happy.

I want to be clear about one thing. Looking bad on the outside is not the goal. That won't make you look more beautiful on the inside. We need to look our best. But, more importantly, there is an inner beauty we must strive for.

Some of the holy women in the Bible were known for their physical beauty as well as their spiritual beauty. Sarah must have been very beautiful. She was taken from Abraham twice by kings. The second time was after Abraham mentioned that she was ninety years old (Genesis 17:17; 20:2). Ninety years old and still beautiful!

Esther must have also been especially beautiful. And she was not only beautiful but she was pampered. She spent a year in beauty treatments and won the beauty contest to be queen.

However, it is Sarah's and Esther's spiritual beauty that lives on. It is imperishable. They trusted God and surrendered their lives to his will.

I want to encourage you to wear your beautiful spiritual garments every day and consider how to spiritually adorn yourself. Don't settle for only the outward. Take the time to consider your inner beauty and what makes you beautiful forever.

Worksheet 3 - Spiritual Adornment

Do you place a high value on reading and studying the Bible?

What is your greatest challenge in having consistent or meaningful study times?

_____

_____

_____

Are you more serious about your inward beauty or your outward beauty?

_____

_____

_____

In what ways do you like to adorn yourself physically?

_____

_____

_____

What qualities make you feel spiritually beautiful?

_____

_____

_____

_____

_____

_____

_____

Memory Verse: 1 Timothy 2:9-10

– Chapter 4 –

Modesty and Decorum

*I also want women to dress modestly [kosmois], with decency
[aidos]...*

1 Timothy 2:9

Now that we have considered spiritual beauty and spiritual adornment, we will next consider our physical adornment and the challenges
we face to be pure in this area of our lives. I want to remind you of
God's promises as you consider this aspect of purity. He promises to
walk with you, live with you and be your Father. Let this motivate you
as you contemplate your purity. Remember that the scriptures about
modesty and decency are not to burden you, but rather to protect you
and help you draw closer to God.

* * *

Physically, we adorn ourselves in many ways. The most basic
adornment is clothing. After Adam and Eve disobeyed God, their first
response was to hide because of their nakedness. We read that they
felt ashamed without clothing and that God made garments for them
before he sent them out of the Garden of Eden (Genesis 3:21). I
imagine that it wasn't long after Eve left the Garden of Eden that she
began to add special touches to her animal skin outfits. She may have
even worn a necklace before she wore clothes! Decorating ourselves is
a very natural part of us.

We adorn just about every part of our bodies. We put colors on our cheeks, eyelids, lips, fingernails, toenails and hair. And we wear jewelry to decorate our ears, neck, fingers, toes, wrists, ankles, hair and other places. And the clothing we wear is specific for the occasion. We even sometimes wear uncomfortable shoes because beauty is more important to us than comfort.

Clothing or a lack of it is mentioned in many stories in the Bible. Examples include Noah's nakedness and the impact it had on his family (Genesis 9:21-25); Rebekah deceiving Isaac by having Jacob put on his brother's clothes (Genesis 27:15); Tamar dressing like a prostitute to deceive her father-in-law (Genesis 38:13-15); and John the Baptist's unusual choice of clothing (Matthew 3:4).

The clothing we choose to wear or not wear says a lot about us. We can actually make a statement by what we wear. If a woman arrived at church wearing a pantsuit, button-down shirt, tie and wingtip shoes, she would be making a strong anti-feminine statement. An all leather outfit would make a different statement, or a lacy blouse and ruffled skirt would make yet another statement.

Fashion is a multi-billion dollar industry, and it's always changing. It is to the designers' financial benefit to change the styles. It keeps them in business. As long as I can remember, there have been do's and don'ts about the latest styles, such as pleats are in or pleats are out; pink is in or it's out. And there are also the old standby rules of fashion to remember, such as don't wear white shoes before Memorial Day or after Labor Day or just don't wear white shoes. Fashion rules are ever changing, but what about the never-changing scriptures? What do they say about our fashion choices? Let's again consider the following passage:

> *I also want women to dress modestly [kosmois], with decency [aidos]...*
>
> 1 Timothy 2:9

The Greek word translated "modestly" is *kosmois.*

Definition: *Kosmios* (kos´-mee-os); orderly, i.e. decorous: of good behavior, modest.[23]

37

Modest means having or showing a moderate opinion of one's own value, abilities, achievements; not forward; behaving, dressing or speaking in a way that is considered proper or decorous; decent; moderate or reasonable; not extreme; quiet and humble in appearance, style, etc.; not pretentious.[24]

1 Timothy 2:9 uses two different words that have to do with modesty. The first one is *kosmios* which is translated modestly, and the second one is *aidos* which is translated decency. Both of these words have to do with modesty. *Aidos* is more about a sense of shame or decency (we will look at *aidos* in the next lesson). *Kosmios* has to do with modesty or decorum.

Decorous or decorum means good taste in behavior, speech, or dress; an act or requirement of polite behavior.[25] For example, how would you feel if you were a bride and one of your bridesmaids wore blue jeans to your wedding instead of the dress you selected for her? Or if you had hired someone to represent your business to the public, how would you feel if they showed up for work wearing wrinkled, dirty clothing? Proper decorum is one way to show respect and honor to other people.

Decorum simply means showing consideration for others. I can do that by what I wear. Not that I am dressing to impress, but I am dressing in a way that says I want to be polite and considerate of you. A modern way to say this is "it's not all about me" in how I dress. Actually, there is no place in a Christian's life that we can say it's all about me. Clothing is no exception.

Generally, there is a stronger sense of decorum in regard to weddings and funerals than most events, but there are numerous other times we need to make sure we are considerate in what we wear. Consider the following scripture in which Jesus spoke of decorum at a wedding. He makes a serious point about proper "spiritual" clothing.

> *"But when the king came in to see the guests, he noticed a man there who was not wearing wedding clothes. 'Friend,' he asked, 'how did you get in here without wedding clothes?' The man was speechless."*

> Matthew 22:11-12

Today many associate decorum with stiffness (uncoolness) or formality. Over the last four decades, our culture has become so casual that proper decorum is often ridiculed. In the 1970's, an anti-establishment theme that was promoted was "do your own thing." It's a theme that has permeated our culture. Yet, 1 Timothy 2:9-10 calls us to dress in a decorous and modest way.

What would modest or decorous look like for Christian women today? It would certainly be different from 100 years ago, and 100 years ago would have been different from 200 years ago. It's a moving standard. Since it's a moving standard, can we just do our own thing? Is decorum really necessary? The Bible can help us with this. There are many verses about being considerate of others. Consider the following scriptures in light of your choice of clothing:

> *Do nothing out of selfish ambition or vain conceit, but in humility consider others better than yourselves.*
>
> Philippians 2:3

> *We who are strong ought to bear with the failings of the weak and not to please ourselves. Each of us should please his neighbor for his good, to build him up.*
>
> Romans 15:1-2

> *For we are taking pains to do what is right, not only in the eyes of the Lord but also in the eyes of men.*
>
> 2 Corinthians 8:21

> *Be devoted to one another in brotherly love. Honor one another above yourselves.*
>
> Romans 12:10

I want to clarify that I'm not suggesting we all go out and buy Emily Post's book on proper etiquette, but I'm not knocking it either. There are many ways we can show consideration to those around us. One of them is by how we dress. That's the point of 1 Timothy 2:9 when it says to dress in a decorous or modest way. As our clothing reflects our personalities, it should also reflect our consideration for others.

Worksheet 4 - Modesty & Decorum

When are times we can show others consideration through our choices?

_____

_____

_____

Does the idea of proper decorum bother you?

Do you see decorum as politeness or stiffness?

How does decorum impact you?

_____

_____

_____

Are there times you feel stronger about proper decorum?

Does it bother you to dress up for special occasions, church services, weddings, funerals, special school functions?

Do you have a strong consideration for other people in your choices? Is there an area in which you need to grow?

_____

_____

_____

_____

_____

_____

_____

_____

Memory Verse: Philippians 2:3 *Do nothing out of selfish ambition or vain conceit, but in humility consider others better than yourselves*

– Chapter 5 –

Decency and Propriety

I also want women to dress modestly, with decency [aidos] and propriety [sophrosyne]...

1 Timothy 2:9

The Greek word translated "decency" is *aidos.*

Definition: *Aidos* (ahee-doce´); a sense of shame or modesty. Shamefastness is modesty which is "fast" or rooted in the character. *Aidos* would always restrain a good man from an unworthy act.[26]

The word *aidos* means having a strong sense of shame. Shame is a painful feeling of having lost the respect of others.[27] The language used in the Greek dictionary is a little archaic when it uses the word shamefastness. "Shame - fast - ness" would mean you keep it close to you. However, women today are taught the opposite of this. We are taught to be bold and never feel ashamed of anything, as though there is something inherently wrong with shame. Now, there can be misdirected shame that we should not have to bear, but shame, in and of itself, is not always bad. The following verse shows that lack of shame is not a new problem:

Are they ashamed of their loathsome conduct? No, they have no shame at all; they do not even know how to blush. So they will fall among the fallen; they will be brought down when they are punished, says the LORD.

Jeremiah 8:12

We don't want to unduly feel shame but we need to feel it if we are out of line with God. We want to remember how to blush.

It's a gradual process that gets us to a point of accepting something that is immodest or indecent. Women wear clothing today that a few years ago they would not have considered wearing outside their bedroom, but now it is a common practice.

A quality that will help us navigate the choices we have in the fashion world is discretion. Discretion will help us make good judgements about what we will wear. It helps us see the bigger picture of the choices -- both physical and spiritual -- that are before us. Consider what the Bible has to say about discretion:

> *Discretion will protect you, and understanding will guard you.*
> Proverbs 2:11

> *Like a gold ring in a pig's snout is a beautiful woman who shows no discretion.*
> Proverbs 11:22

Can you picture a pig with a gold snout ring? It will soon be covered with mud. What a waste! Beauty without discretion is the same. This is why we are told to dress with decency and propriety.

The Greek word translated "propriety" is *sophrosyne.*

Definition: *Sophrosyne* (so-fros-oo´-nay); sound judgment. It is that habitual inner self-government, with its constant rein on all passions and desires, enabling the believer to be conformed to the mind of Christ. Its root word is *sophrono* which is translated soberminded or safe or sound in mind; moderate as to opinion or passion; discreet, temperate.[28]

Propriety is the English word used to translate *sophrosyne*, but we don't use this word much today. Many would probably have a difficult time defining propriety. Propriety means the quality of being proper or to conform to what is proper.[29] However, this falls short of expressing what *sophrosyne* means. Although *sophrosyne* leads you to doing what is proper, it has a much deeper meaning. It has to do with what you allow yourself to think about – having a constant rein on your desires and passions. And this is self-government, not pressure from others to conform.

With *sophrosyne* we can turn our thoughts away from things that might be harmful to us, things such as worry, self-hatred or jealousy. With a "constant rein on all passions and desires," you can control an angry thought and not say something improper. On the outside you did what was proper, but you were using restraint on a much deeper level.

Sophrosyne will help you exercise self-restraint as you choose your clothing. Is it decent? Is this something a godly woman would wear, or am I caught up in "fashionable" indecency?

Who started these styles anyway? Was it a godly woman or was it a young rock star who is marketing her music to people in the sex, drugs, and rock and roll audience? Who are we following? Sound judgment is what we need to help us think through our choices of fashion. It will help us see when we begin to slip into something that we should not. And sound judgment will help us as we look at areas that are more difficult to decide. We can mistakenly find comfort in our styles because they are not on the latest edge of fashion, but we fail to realize the edge has moved far beyond what is decent. We need sound judgment when it comes to deciding if we will wear the latest fashions.

Sexy vs. Beautiful

I want to stress that dressing decently doesn't mean you have to wear ugly clothing. We can wear beautiful (or stylish) clothing without dressing in a sexy way.

There are lots of ways to be sexy. Sexy can be the way you walk, talk or dress. Are you discrete about when to look sexy? If you are married, when do you dress the most sexy? Is it around your husband? Do you dress in a sexy way for dates with your husband? How about what you wear around the house or your sleepwear? You have it backwards if you dress sexily for work or when you are out with your girlfriends, but wear sweats around your husband.

* * *

43

It is important to understand that men are sexually stimulated by what they see, and women are stimulated more by what they think about and through their emotions. Christian men have to learn to look away from a woman who is dressed in a sexy or provocative way. If you are dressed indecently, you can become an obstacle for a godly man. You are also an obstacle for an ungodly man, but he will look at you anyway.

Sophrosyne will help us dress appropriately for the occasion. It will help us be aware of the men around us and be considerate of them.

> *We put no stumbling block in anyone's path, so that our ministry will not be discredited. Rather, as servants of God we commend ourselves in every way...in purity...*
>
> 2 Corinthians 6:3-6

As servants of God, we must make sure we are not creating a stumbling block by the way we dress. Is your clothing decent? On a typical day, if a Christian man looked at you, would he need to look away to keep from being tempted? I've heard women say, "It's his problem, not mine." But that is not what the scriptures teach. The scriptures teach us to set an example in purity (1 Timothy 4:12), and in the above scripture, we are also told to live a pure life that is commendable. Can you be commended for your discretion and decency?

You may be wondering, "Does it really matter?" "Is this really worthy of our consideration?" Yes to both questions!

> *"Woe to the world because of the things that cause people to sin! Such things must come, but woe to the man through whom they come! If your hand or your foot causes you to sin cut it off and throw it away. It is better for you to enter life maimed or crippled than to have two hands or two feet and be thrown into eternal fire. And if your eye causes you to sin, gouge it out and throw it away. It is better for you to enter life with one eye than to have two eyes and be thrown into the fire of hell."*
>
> Matthew 18:7-9

This scripture explains that we have a responsibility to those around us, and that we should take a radical approach to anything that would cause us to sin or that might cause someone else to sin.

About fifteen years ago, a young single mom began Bible studies and soon became a Christian. As her convictions grew through her studies, she realized she did not dress the way a Christian would dress. She went home and sifted through her clothes to determine what to get rid of. As she was sorting them, she decided to throw away anything that was indecent, because she did not want to encourage anyone else to wear it. Today she is a beautiful woman who is known for her godly life. She took a radical approach to her obedience and God has blessed her life in many ways.

Our outward clothing is only one step to purity, but it is a very important one. We must understand how visually stimulating these things are to men. Take time to consider your wardrobe, seek advice and pray about this. Remember that the Spirit will lead you.

Worksheet 5 - Decency and Propriety

Do you have a strong sense of decency in your clothing?

Is it part of your character or is this something you have had to develop as a Christian?

_____

_____

_____

Do you wear clothes today you would have considered immodest five to ten years ago?

Who influences your fashion choices the most?

_____

_____

Consider your clothing for a minute. Would you describe your clothing as sexy? (If you don't know, ask a friend who will give you an honest answer.)

_____

_____

If you are married, when and where do you wear your sexiest clothing?

_____

_____

_____

_____

_____

_____

_____

Memory Verse: Proverbs 11:22

– Chapter 6 –

Motives of the Heart

All a man's ways seem innocent to him, but motives are weighed by the LORD.

Proverbs 16:2

Therefore judge nothing before the appointed time; wait till the Lord comes. He will bring to light what is hidden in darkness and will expose the motives of men's hearts. At that time each will receive his praise from God.

1 Corinthians 4:5

Our motives count before God, so it's important for us to consider the "why" behind our choices. In the previous chapter we looked at the Greek word *sophrosyne* which is translated propriety. Propriety (*sophrosyne*) will help us go deeper than just deciding whether something is decent. It will help us with the deeper issue of why do I want to wear something that may not be decent. There are three motives I want to address concerning our choice of clothing: 1) ego building, 2) power and prestige, and 3) approval or praise. These are closely linked. They all focus on self, but they are three distinct areas we need to consider.

Ego building

Clothing can build up our egos. We can either feel confident or deflated just because of the clothing we are wearing. Recently my husband and I hosted several couples for an evening. When one of the couples arrived, the wife looked especially beautiful. She had styled her hair and wore a beautiful outfit. Many of the women commented on how beautiful she looked. Later that week, she told me that it took everything in her to be gracious and accept the compliments because she felt self-conscious about her shoes. She thought they were ugly. By the time she was telling me the story, she thought it was funny, but when she was in the middle of it, she wasn't laughing. She was feeling deflated by ugly shoes. She almost let this wonderful evening get away from her. Fortunately, she worked through it.

I've felt embarrassed by clothing and shoes before. An ego can be a powerful force to deal with and can bring out our insecurities. Most of us are insecure to some extent. Even the most beautiful women can have deep insecurities about themselves and how they look. Insecurity about how we look can fill us with worry and anxiety and make us miserable. During these times, it is unlikely that you will be giving to other people, because your focus is on yourself.

If you are insecure, you may find that you compare yourself to other women. This can lead to sins such as jealousy and envy. Deep insecurity can lead us to be obsessed about the world's idea of beauty and can also be the cause of eating disorders. It can also lead us to wearing clothing that is indecent.

Sophrosyne will help us get through the challenge of wearing clothing to build our own ego. We must think spiritually to overcome this kind of insecurity. As Christian women, we have set our sights on a greater goal than just physical beauty -- we want to be beautiful to God, too.

Power and Prestige

Clothing can give us a sense of power and prestige. It is a power that can open doors. For a young girl, it may be that she has the admiration of the other girls in her class because she always has the latest styles. She may be "popular." She may also have the attention of the boys around her. But no matter what our age, being able to turn a man's head gives us a feeling of power.

"Girl power" is a modern day mantra, but women have known this from the beginning. Why did Eve eat the forbidden fruit? Because Satan tempted her with being like God. The fact that Adam chose to eat it with her instead of obeying God shows Eve's power in her relationship with Adam.

Another example that illustrates a woman's power and prestige is the story of Esther. She needed to get her husband, the king, to make a ruling that would save the Jewish people, but for thirty days he had not called for her. She had one option – show up unannounced. It was a dangerous move. If he did not hold out the golden scepter, she would lose her life (Esther 4:11).

The Bible simply states that before she went to see the king, she put on her royal robes. I'm sure this is an understatement! I don't think she just threw on a pretty dress. She knew how to dress to get the king's attention.

Before she became queen, she went through a year of beauty treatments. And when it was her turn to meet the king for the first time, she could have picked anything she wanted from the closets of the harem (Esther 2:13). She wisely asked for advice on what to wear, and she won the favor of the king. In fact, she won the favor of everyone who saw her (Esther 2:15).

I believe Esther wanted to win this beauty contest. If she had not become queen, she would have spent the rest of her life in the king's harem. The custom was that when an order was sent to a family for a young woman to go to the palace, the parents, however unwilling, dared not refuse the honor for their daughter. Although they knew that they would never see her again once she was in the royal harem, they were obliged to yield a silent and passive compliance.[30] Becoming queen sounded like a much better alternative. And she did.

Later when she was getting ready to go before the king unannounced, she got dressed up! When the king saw her standing there, he reached out his golden scepter and she walked up and touched it. He was so smitten by her that he offered her anything she wanted, up to half of his vast kingdom. This is a red carpet entrance that made history!

Esther turned her husband's head by putting on her royal robes, but she also made herself spiritually beautiful. She had fasted and prayed for three days seeking God's help in this challenging time. She wasn't relying only on her physical beauty and beautiful clothing, she was also spiritually clothed with strength.

> *She is clothed with strength and dignity; she can laugh at the days to come.*
>
> Proverbs 31:25

Although "girl power" is available to us, there is greater strength in spiritual beauty. Women who try to gain power by becoming worldly pay a big price and can lose their dignity. We have all seen beautiful, talented women who have lost their dignity while using their beauty to gain something. Strength and dignity do not define their lives.

Another strength of spiritual beauty is being able to laugh at the days to come. This means you are not stressed out by life. Instead you are trusting God and enjoying your life. This is true power.

Approval and Praise

Do you seek approval in the clothes you wear? Are you an approval and praise "junkie"? You are if you feel good or bad about yourself depending on whether or not someone compliments you. This is just another way our insecurities can attack us.

Approval or praise can actually feel pretty good! I've noticed on many occasions that approval flows through women's conversations in the form of compliments. And a nice compliment about how you look can lift your spirit.

Last year I spent a weekend with three of my girlfriends. I had just begun my study of spiritual beauty and purity, so I was more aware of compliments than usual. It was eye-opening to me to see how much we complimented each other during the weekend. Our conversations were salted with compliments about each other's clothing, shoes, purses, hairstyles, jewelry, etc.

Expressing approval about each other's choices is a very natural response, but we need to be careful that approval and praise is not our goal. Trying to find security in our lives through the approval and praise of others can leave us empty. It can also lead us to things that are ungodly, including wearing things that are not decent.

Sophrosyne (a constant rein on our passions and desires) will help us overcome these insecurities. It will help us develop confidence in who we are and what standard we will hold to in our lives. When I find that I'm insecure, I ask myself, "Who am I trying to please?" This helps me overcome my insecurities and focus on what is really important.

In the choices we have before us, we want to make sure that we are seeking God's approval first and not conforming to worldly standards. The following verse tells us how to gain the right kind of approval:

> *Charm is deceptive, and beauty is fleeting; but a woman who fears the LORD is to be praised. Give her the reward she has earned, and let her works bring her praise at the city gate.*
>
> Proverbs 31:30-31

One More Thing

There can be a lot of pressure on us regarding our appearance. This is true of older women as well as young teens. According to the Dove study, older women today feel that they are expected to be more attractive than their mothers were at the same age.[31] So no matter what our age, the why behind what we wear is important to consider. Becoming spiritually beautiful is lasting, unfading and fulfilling. Beauty driven by insecurities can leave you empty.

I want to stress that I'm not saying you should wear dowdy, unflattering clothing. Dress in beautiful, flattering clothing. You can dress beautifully or tastefully without being immodest or indecent. Sometimes it can be difficult to know, so it's always good to check your heart and get some advice if it's unclear to you. Let's be known especially for our spiritual beauty.

> *Set your minds on things above, not on earthly things. For you died, and your life is now hidden with Christ in God. When Christ, who is your life, appears, then you also will appear with him in glory. Put to death, therefore, whatever belongs to your earthly nature: sexual immorality, impurity, lust, evil desires and greed, which is idolatry.*
>
> Colossians 3:2-5

Promise:
You will appear with
him in glory.

Worksheet 6 - Motives of the Heart

Do you tend to be insecure in how you look?

Is there something in fashion to which you look to fill an insecurity in you? If so, what?

_____

_____

_____

_____

_____

_____

Do you look to fashion to build your ego?

Do you feel more powerful or prestigious by what you wear?

Do you look for approval and praise in what you wear?

What motivates your choice of clothing?

_____

_____

_____

_____

_____

_____

_____

_____

_____

_____

_____

Memory Verse: Psalms 51:10

– Chapter 7 –

Protecting Our Daughters

Then they can train the younger women...to be self-controlled and pure...

Titus 2:4-5

The story of Dinah, Jacob's only daughter, is a tragic event in the history of the Israelites (Genesis 34). When she visited the women of the nearby city, she was raped by a man whose father ruled the area. Two of her brothers responded by murdering all the men in the city. Then the family was forced to move. Years later when Jacob was about to die, these two brothers did not receive a blessing from him because of their violent behavior. Instead, they received a curse (Genesis 49:5-7).

The results of Dinah's tragedy unfolded over many years. The tragedy of a young girl being violated can go on for a long time -- even a lifetime. And it not only affects her, but also her family.

I want to know how this happened to Dinah. Why did her family allow her to go unchaperoned to this city? Did they think it was safe in this pagan community? Did they let her go because she insisted she could take care of herself?

There are a lot of unanswered questions in this story. Perhaps this was a onetime bad judgment made by her parents, or maybe they were somehow lulled into a sense of safety in an unsafe place. Today teen girls face many challenges regarding purity and we need to take these challenges very seriously.

Recently on my way home from work, I sat beside a group of young girls (probably 13-14 years old) on the commuter train. They had spent the day in the city and were on their way home. They unabashedly discussed parties and "making out" with boys. The level of impurity in their lives made me so sad. I thought about the impact this would have on them, and I wondered about their lives in the years to come. They have no understanding of the impact these things will have on them.

The following quote from *Why the Sexualization of Childhood Is Harmful for Children* explains how the focus on sexuality impacts children:

> It is not the fact that children are learning about sex when they are young that is a problem, the problem is what today's sexualized environment is teaching them. Children's ideas about what it means to be a boy and girl and about the nature of sex and sexuality develop gradually and are greatly influenced by the information the environment provides. The popular culture of today bombards girls with large doses of sexual content that they cannot understand and that can even scare them. It provides them with a very narrow definition of femaleness and sexuality that focuses them primarily on appearance. Their value is determined by how well they succeed at meeting the sexualized ideal. It can also promote precocious sexual behavior before they have an understanding of the deeper meanings of the behavior. When children are young, long before they can fully understand the meaning of sex and sexual relations, we should be laying the foundation for later healthy sexual relationships. And unless we begin to deal more proactively with the disconnect between what children need and what they are getting today, it does not bode well for the future of intimate and caring relationships in which sex is a part, when today's children grow up.[32]

One of the greatest challenges parents face to counteract today's sexualized environment is television. While you teach your daughter godly values, many movies or television shows promote premarital sex as a normal part of growing up. The following *Chicago Tribune* article shows how young girls can be influenced by older movie stars:

Multiple posters of Disney teen queen Hilary Duff decorate the bedroom of my 7-year-old daughter, a "Lizzie McGuire" fan going way back to when she was 6. There's sweet smiling Hil in the pink sweater. There's butter-haired Hil looking over her shoulder. There's Hil with the sleeveless top and choker necklace.

These are the welcomed Hilarys, the ones who evoke the Disney Channel's hit show (2001-2004), featuring the likable, effervescent junior high student, her two best friends, clueless parents and a bratty little brother. Lizzie's high jinks at home and school made her – and Duff – an idol for tweeners and pretweens like my daughter, Anika.

But now there's a new Hil, one whom oglers might call Hil-a-*ray, baby,* she of the knowing look, smoldering eyes, hollowed-out cheeks and exposed cleavage. This Hil is gazing upon my daughter, and my daughter is gazing right back.

I do not want this Hilary in my house.[33]

This mom is seeing before her eyes the transformation of her young daughter's TV idol. There is a Hollywood formula for girl stars like Britney Spears, Lindsay Lohan and Hilary Duff. They market to young fans of the Mickey Mouse Club or Disney Channel, and then when these stars become 18, there is a continuing effort to pull these young fans along with the older version of this star. It is a marketing ploy that brings in big bucks. What little girl doesn't want to dress like a star, sing like a star, or dance like a star! Meanwhile their "star" is trying to become the next sex symbol in Hollywood.

Several years ago I had a discussion with a neighbor about her plans to take her young daughter to a Britney Spears concert. This was the year that Britney turned 18. I was surprised that she took her young daughter to this concert, but her daughter really wanted to go. After the concert, my neighbor was a little concerned about all the provocative dance moves her young daughter was doing. This mom had been hooked by the Hollywood marketing campaign that was aimed directly at her young daughter.

The *Trib* article went on to say:

"Most parents say, she's just changing her image, she's sexy now," says Dr. Don Shifrin, chairman of the American Academy of Pediatrics committee on communications, which puts out policy statements on children and the media. "It's like air pollution that we don't notice until we're choking." And whether the "pollution" is coming from Hollywood or Madison Avenue, there's no way to censor the media, Shifrin says. So parents must filter media.

Liz Perle, editor in chief of Common Sense Media, an organization that helps families make media choices, agrees. "There's a heavy burden on parents to manage the messaging," she says. "You can no longer just let them see their idols go through these moments unattended. You can't cover their eyes, so we have to teach them..."

Children can be very accepting of their parents' reasoning, Perle says, however, "they also are going to push back. But you need to say: 'I don't think she is a good role model for you.'"

Media critic Jean Kilbourne, author of the forthcoming book "So Sexy So Soon: The Sexualization of Childhood," says keeping your child safe from images that are taken from "the world of pornography" is paramount. "You do your best to make her understand, and if she doesn't understand you, take [the poster] down. It's the same as if she put an Absolut vodka poster on her wall. You'd take it down."[34]

* * *

Sexy is the "in" look for teens' clothing. There are entire stores that are extremely popular with the younger crowd that have little to offer in the way of decent clothing. Even young girls in first grade can choose sexy clothes. A friend recently told me that her 6-year-old daughter was asking for a short top to show off her bare waist because her friends wore them. The mom lovingly explained to her daughter why she couldn't have it. She went on to explain to her what the boys would think. After her explanation, her daughter was completely in agreement with her mom.

This is exactly what she needed to do. She took the time to explain why. You must equip your child with necessary knowledge about sexuality so they can navigate their world successfully. If you don't explain these things, she will hear about it anyway, but you will not be the one who helped her shape her thinking. Her peers, television shows and movies will be her guide.

Every Young Woman's Battle by Shannon Ethridge discusses sexual purity from emotional, mental, spiritual, and physical perspectives, teaching young women readers to guard their minds, hearts, and bodies in this sex-saturated world. It uses very frank, contemporary language, written especially for young women in their teens to early twenties. I highly recommend this book to moms who are trying to help their daughters with their purity. I recommend you read it with your teen daughter so you can build upon your relationship and can discuss the issues she is facing. (If your daughter is a young teen, you may want to preview it to determine if it's too advanced for her.)

It's important to help young girls and teen girls to understand the difference between beautiful and sexy. They need to be informed. Help them understand that being pure does not mean they are weak or stupid. When we follow the crowd, we are weak. Purity gives us strength.

> *These commandments that I give you today are to be upon your hearts. Impress them on your children. Talk about them when you sit at home and when you walk along the road, when you lie down and when you get up.*
>
> Deuteronomy 6:6-7

Worksheet 7 - Protecting Our Daughters

Do you have a daughter or granddaughter? What are some of the challenges that she faces to be pure?

What will help her to be pure as she faces these challenges?

Memory Verse: Deuteronomy 6:6-7

– Chapter 8 –

Pure Entertainment

Entertainment is something that pleases or amuses us. It can be soothing music, a nail-biting drama, or a competitive sports game. It can be something you enjoy as a participant (or a virtual participant through computers) or just as a fan. There are many ways, godly and ungodly, to be entertained.

When you consider the time spent and all the possibilities, this is another area of our lives that we need to be careful to purify. The following passage explains why we should be different from the world in our choices:

> *Therefore, since Christ suffered in his body, arm yourselves also with the same attitude, because he who has suffered in his body is done with sin. As a result, he does not live the rest of his earthly life for evil human desires, but rather for the will of God. For you have spent enough time in the past doing what pagans choose to do--living in debauchery, lust, drunkenness, orgies, carousing and detestable idolatry.*
>
> 1 Peter 4:1-3

Our relationship with Jesus is the foundation for everything we choose. This is especially true about our entertainment, because our entertainment is something that pleases or amuses us. How you choose to be entertained says a lot about your heart.

Just like the moving standard of decency in clothing, the standard of what is morally acceptable in movies, television, music, books, video games, etc., seems to erode on a yearly basis. The original intent of the movie industry was to provide wholesome entertainment. The following is an excerpt from the Motion Picture Production Code written in the 1930's:

> No picture shall be produced that will lower the moral standards of those who see it. Hence the sympathy of the audience should never be thrown to the side of crime, wrongdoing, evil or sin
>
> These shall never be presented in such a way as to throw sympathy with the crime as against law and justice or to inspire others with a desire for imitation.
>
> The sanctity of the institution of marriage and the home shall be upheld. Pictures shall not infer that low forms of sexual relationships are the accepted or common thing.
>
> Indecent or undue exposure is forbidden.[35]

Obviously, these standards no longer guide the motion picture industry. Some cartoons don't even live up to these standards. We can find ourselves pulled into the fray, laughing at impurity and rooting for someone to get together in an immoral relationship. It's a rare movie that does not have a scene or a theme of immoral sex somewhere in the plot. Even if the movie is about a grand theme, there is often an immoral relationship that is romanticized.

We need to consider carefully what we call entertainment and what God might think about our choices. For example, what about movies and television that promote homosexuality, adultery or sex before marriage? Can you imagine Jesus laughing at the punch lines? I can't because Genesis 6:5 says that man's wickedness grieves God. How can we laugh at something that grieves him? How can we call it entertainment? Our criteria needs to be broader than the question, "Will I struggle with impurity if I watch this." We need to also consider whether God would want us to watch it.

I enjoy watching movies about romance, heros, drama and comedy. I love to watch an underdog be victorious. However, I watch fewer and fewer of today's television and movies because of the immoral themes.

The Apostle Paul makes a statement in 1 Corinthians 5:9-10 that if you tried to completely disassociate yourself from immoral people, you would have to leave this world. So practically speaking, we can't do that, but we can make godly choices about entertainment. Consider what Paul says in the following passage about ungodliness and how to think about it in our own lives:

> *For you were once darkness, but now you are light in the Lord. Live as children of light (for the fruit of the light consists in all goodness, righteousness and truth) and find out what pleases the Lord. Have nothing to do with the fruitless deeds of darkness, but rather expose them. For it is shameful even to mention what the disobedient do in secret.*
>
> Ephesians 5:8-12

* * *

Another way entertainment standards have slipped is the latest wave of forensic science, crime-solving formats. Many of these new shows feature gruesome shots of women being brutalized and terrorized in very graphic and extended ways. Following is an excerpt from an article titled, "TV Terror":

> The look of sheer terror in the woman's eyes is enough to make even the strongest stomach clench. When she realizes she has been kidnapped and can't get out of her captor's car, her eyes futilely dart to the left and to the right. She shouts and whack – a hard slap comes slamming across her face. The end seems near. Yet the writers of the new CBS drama "Criminal Minds" take the slow torture of an attractive, young female victim as something to be drawn out ever so slowly.
>
> Jeffrey Sconce, an associate professor of radio, television and film at Northwestern University says, "Sadistic is the only word to use for some of these shows..."[36]

If you compare these television shows today with five or ten years ago, you can see how much the standards regarding violence have declined. The following verses explain that we can actually crave violence:

> *From the fruit of his lips a man enjoys good things, but the unfaithful have a craving for violence.*
>
> Proverbs 13:2

> *Having lost all sensitivity, they have given themselves over to sensuality so as to indulge in every kind of impurity, with a continual lust for more.*
>
> Ephesians 4:19

We can see why standards erode. The more we sin, the less sensitivity we have to what is evil. The following verse shows how God feels about those who love violence:

> *The LORD examines the righteous, but the wicked and those who love violence his soul hates.*
>
> Psalms 11:5

* * *

Another area we must consider is pornography. Pornography is anything that is viewed for sexual arousal. It is a $57 billion industry worldwide. Porn revenue is larger than all combined revenues of all professional football, baseball and basketball franchises.[37] Pornography is more than conveniently available, it is difficult to keep out of your home if you have television or internet access.

Pornography is dangerous and destructive and it has destroyed many families. It is like a drug that demands more and more. Today many people face additions to pornography and this addiction has serious consequences in their lives. One danger of pornography is that it can destroy the intimacy of a marriage (or a future marriage). If you are married and you watch sexy or pornographic movies to "get in the mood," you are doing damage to your intimacy as a couple. (More about this later.)

The Internet

The internet, although a great resource for us, has little or no censoring. It is estimated that there are over 4.2 million pornographic websites that generate $2.5 billion in revenues.[38]

There are many other temptations on the internet. One temptation that can seem harmless is the social appeal. Chat rooms can have quite a pull for a woman who is lonely. However, chat rooms are such a poor way to build a relationship, because you get a distorted view of the person with whom you are chatting. There is no accountability for what is said, and you have no idea about their reputation. It is a dangerous way to attempt to make social connections. One problem is that you can get emotionally involved before you really know the person. Movies such as *You've Got Mail* have glamorized the internet connection, but that is not the real world of the internet. A real relationship has to be built in person.

* * *

If you have children, be sure that you are aware of their computer use. I've known parents who had stricter rules about telephone use than their children's computer use. If you don't understand the internet and your child uses it regularly, you need to get up-to-date about *My Space* and similar sites and the obstacles children face because of this media. Would you allow your child to talk with a total stranger for a long period on the telephone? I think not. You need to know who they are chatting with on the internet, too.

The internet offers us some wonderful resources, but be aware of the hazards of this communications medium.

* * *

We have enough of a battle with the world without subjecting ourselves to ungodly entertainment. We need to carefully consider our entertainment.

> *I will set before my eyes no vile thing. The deeds of faithless men I hate; they will not cling to me. Men of perverse heart shall be far from me; I will have nothing to do with evil.*
> Psalms 101:3-4

Worksheet 8 - Pure Entertainment

What are your guidelines for entertainment?

Have you seen your own standards slip in any way concerning your choice of music, movies or television?

What scriptures help you the most when it comes to choosing your entertainment?

Memory Verse: Psalms 101:3-4

– Chapter 9 –

Sexual Purity

But among you there must not be even a hint of sexual immorality, or of any kind of impurity, or of greed, because these are improper for God's holy people.

Ephesians 5:3

Many people are misinformed about sexual immorality and impurity. Some who claim to be Christians say that as long as you love each other premarital sex is not a sin. Others have a very narrow definition of adultery and believe that technically they have not committed adultery even though they had a sexual encounter with someone who is not their spouse. But let's consider how Jesus defined adultery:

You have heard that it was said, "Do not commit adultery."
But I tell you that anyone who looks at a woman lustfully has already committed adultery with her in his heart.

Matthew 5:27-28

Jesus defined adultery more broadly than the physical act. He explains in this verse:

For out of the heart come evil thoughts, murder, adultery, sexual immorality, theft, false testimony, slander.

Matthew 15:19

Jesus gives us an important insight into the heart -- this is where sin begins, including sexual sins. Purifying our hearts is as important as purifying our actions. 1 Corinthians 7:1 tells us to purify both body and spirit. We must purify not only our outward actions, but also our thoughts (mind) and emotional longings (heart).

I find this good and bad news. Bad news because I'm guilty of a lot more sin than I initially thought I was, and good news because now I know how to fight this battle for purity. If we want to purify something that is polluted, whether it be air, water or land, it is more effective to work on the source of the problem rather than a symptom. The source of sexual impurity is the heart, so that's where we need to begin. However, the following scripture tells us that our hearts present a special challenge:

> *The heart is deceitful above all things and beyond cure. Who can understand it?*
>
> Jeremiah 17:9

We can be deceived by our own hearts. This means we accept something for truth that is a lie. But this does not mean we are without hope, because this is another area in which God's word will help us.

> *For the word of God is living and active. Sharper than any double-edged sword, it penetrates even to dividing soul and spirit, joints and marrow; it judges the thoughts and attitudes of the heart.* [Emphasis added.]
>
> Hebrews 4:12

Without God, we could not understand our hearts, but with the help of his word, we can judge what is in our hearts and begin to purify them. Let's consider some of the deceptions we face regarding sexual impurity and what the Bible has to say about these deceptions. Following are a few that are common:

- I can handle this temptation.
- It doesn't hurt anyone.
- It's my business what I do.
- It's not really that bad.
- At least I'm not as bad as some people.

These deceptions are dangerous because, if we believe them, we will face consequences both now and later. These consequences are eternal, physical and emotional.

Eternal Consequences

Put to death, therefore, whatever belongs to your earthly nature: sexual immorality, impurity, lust, evil desires and greed, which is idolatry. Because of these, the wrath of God is coming.

Colossians 3:5-6

Therefore, get rid of all moral filth and the evil that is so prevalent and humbly accept the word planted in you, which can save you.

James 1:21

There are many warnings and promises in the Bible about our eternal destiny. The following scriptures give a very specific list of sexual sins that can have eternal consequences:

The acts of the sinful nature are obvious: sexual immorality [moicheia] [porneia], impurity [akatharsia] and debauchery [aselgeia]... I warn you, as I did before, that those who live like this will not inherit the kingdom of God.

Galatians 5:19-21

Do you not know that the wicked will not inherit the kingdom of God? Do not be deceived: Neither the sexually immoral [pornos] nor idolaters nor adulterers [moichos] nor male prostitutes nor homosexual offenders [arsenokoitēs] nor thieves nor the greedy nor drunkards nor slanderers nor swindlers will inherit the kingdom of God.

1 Corinthians 6:9-10

To better understand these scriptures, consider the meanings of the Greek words shown above in brackets:

- Adultery (*moicheia* and *moichos*) specifically means voluntary sexual intercourse between a man and woman who are not married to each other and where one or both are married to another person.

- Sexual immorality (*porneia* and *pornos*) is a broader definition than *moicheia* and *moichos*. It includes adultery, incest and any voluntary sexual intercourse between a man and a woman who are not married to each other.

- Impurity (*akatharsia*) means physical or moral uncleanness. This would include voluntary behavior with another person outside of marriage that is sexual in nature.

- Debauchery (*aselgeia*) means that which is an insolent (boldly disrespectful) disregard of decency and an absence of restraint.

- Homosexual offenders (*arsenokoitēs*) means men having sex with men and women having sex with women.[39]

The Bible states that sexual immorality and impurity are obvious sins, and if we live this way, we will not inherit the kingdom of heaven. But eternal consequences can seem unreal. First, they are experienced after death. It is only by faith that we act upon this warning. Second, we have been influenced by worldly thinking. The world asks, "How can a loving God send someone to hell?" So they reason God will not judge them and they deliberately keep on sinning.

It is true that God is loving. In fact, he so loved us that he was willing to give up his only son in order for us to come into a relationship with him (John 3:16). But to think we do not need to obey is a dangerous deception.

> *If we deliberately keep on sinning after we have received the knowledge of the truth, no sacrifice for sins is left, but only a fearful expectation of judgment and of raging fire that will consume the enemies of God.*
>
> Hebrews 10:26-27

True Christians cannot have even a hint of sexual immorality or impurity in their lives (Ephesians 5:3). This is a hard-line teaching, but obeying it protects us not only from eternal consequences, but also from physical and emotional consequences.

Physical Consequences

One of the deceptions regarding sexual impurity is that it doesn't hurt anybody. Consider these biblical warnings:

> *Flee from sexual immorality. All other sins a man commits are outside his body, but he who sins sexually sins against his own body.*
>
> 1 Corinthians 6:18

> *Therefore God gave them over in the sinful desires of their hearts to sexual impurity for the degrading of their bodies with one another.*
>
> Romans 1:24

Sexual immorality is actually a sin against your own body. This is evident from the damage caused by sexually transmitted diseases. STDs can cause infections of the reproductive organs, including infertility, ectopic pregnancy, abscess formation, chronic pelvic pain, cancer and even death. The consequences of STDs can be devastating and long-term. Although substantial progress has been made in the prevention, diagnoses, and treatment of certain STDs, an estimated 19 million new infections occur every year in the U.S.

Human papillomavirus, or HPV, is the name of a group of viruses that includes more than 100 different strains. More than 30 of these viruses are sexually transmitted. There are about 20 million people who are currently infected with HPV, and every year in the U.S., about 6.2 million people get HPV. It is the major cause of cervical cancer.[40]

The most talked about STD around the world is HIV/AIDS. Globally, over 25 million people have died of AIDS since 1981, and an estimated 33 to 46 million people are living with HIV/AIDS.[41]

Another consequence of sexual impurity is an unwanted pregnancy. This can change the course of a woman's life. She may feel forced into a quick marriage, or she may choose to raise her child by herself and face the challenges of being a single mom. She may give up her child for adoption and suffer many emotional challenges for years. Or she may add another sin to her life (along with a lot of emotional pain) by ending her unborn child's life by abortion. Since abortion was legalized in 1973, over 47 million women in the United States have had an abortion.[42]

* * *

Sexual impurity has serious physical consequences. This is another example of how God offers us safety through his wisdom. God is not giving us burdensome rules to follow -- sexual purity will protect us.

"For the waywardness of the simple will kill them, and the complacency of fools will destroy them; but whoever listens to me will live in safety and be at ease, without fear of harm."
Proverbs 1:32-33

God created Adam and Eve to live in a monogamous relationship (Genesis 2:24). Jesus explained this in the following verse:

> *"Haven't you read," he replied, "that at the beginning the Creator 'made them male and female,' and said, 'For this reason a man will leave his father and mother and be united to his wife, and the two will become one flesh'? So they are no longer two, but one. Therefore what God has joined together, let man not separate."*
>
> Matthew 19:4-6

Even the Centers for Disease Control and Prevention advises living in a long-term, mutually monogamous relationship to prevent STDs. It is false security to think that safe sexual practices will prevent all STDs. The CDC says an HPV infection can occur in both male and female genital areas even if they are covered or protected by a latex condom, as well as in areas that are not covered. It is estimated that at least 50 percent of sexually active men and women will acquire a genital HPV infection at some point in their lives.[43]

There are many physical challenges and hardships that sexual impurity can bring. When someone says that sexual impurity doesn't hurt anybody, they are deceived.

Emotional Consequences

One of the many emotional consequences of sexual impurity is that we do not get to enjoy the fruit of the Holy Spirit. As you read the following passage, contrast the emotional consequences of the sins listed below with the emotions we enjoy through the qualities of the Holy Spirit.

> *The acts of the sinful nature are obvious: sexual immorality, impurity and debauchery; idolatry and witchcraft; hatred, discord, jealousy, fits of rage, selfish ambition, dissensions, factions and envy; drunkenness, orgies, and the like. I warn you, as I did before, that those who live like this will not inherit the kingdom of God. But the fruit of the Spirit is love, joy, peace, patience, kindness, goodness, faithfulness, gentleness and self-control. Against such things there is no law. Those who belong to Christ Jesus have crucified the sinful nature with its passions*

71

and desires. Since we live by the Spirit, let us keep in step with
the Spirit. [Emphasis added.]

Galatians 5:22-24

Sin has enormous emotional consequences. It robs us of these wonderful qualities. To enjoy the fruit of the Holy Spirit in our lives, we must crucify our sinful nature with its passions and desires. To do this, we need to understand our emotional longings and how they can lead to impurity or moral uncleanness and the consequences these things bring into our lives.

While most men are tempted visually, women are more apt to be tempted through their emotions. Movies we call "chick flicks" show the knight in shining armor or prince charming rescuing the damsel in distress. My personal favorite is the story of Cinderella. In the end of the story, Cinderella marries her prince. What if after Cinderella married the prince, she began to imagine herself with another man or she found herself being drawn in her heart to another man? That would be a terrible ending! She is supposed to live "happily ever after" with the prince. I would call a story like that a tragedy.

Book sales also indicate how much women are drawn by their emotional longings to the knight-in-shining-armor kind of guy. Romance books generated $1.2 billion in sales in 2004, and 78% of the 64.6 million Americans who read at least one romance novel were women.[44]

I am not suggesting that a Christian should not watch romantic movies or read a romantic book, but we need to understand why these are attractive to us and the impact they can have on us and how they can tempt us. A married woman may be tempted to turn to these things as a substitute for an emotional connection with her husband. A common deception is that an affair of the heart is no big deal and that no one gets hurt. However, if we do not restrain ungodly thoughts and desires, we will face serious consequences -- like not enjoying the fruit of the Holy Spirit in our lives.

Another consequence if you are married is that an affair of the heart will damage your intimacy as a couple. You cannot be one with your husband and be intimately connected to him when you are giving a part of your heart to someone else. Oneness in marriage involves our emotions and thoughts as well as our physical relationship.

This means we must be pure emotionally, mentally and physically. If you are married, your husband is the only one you have sexual thoughts about, and he is the only one with whom you have sex. Emotional and mental purity would mean you guard your feelings and thoughts concerning other men, and you do not fantasize about being with another man.

At the beginning of this book, I said that God did not give us a legalistic list of rules to follow just to put us to the test. Instead, he is giving us the inside scoop on how to have a glorious life. For instance, which would you rather have in your marriage:

1)   When you spend time together sexually, you are thinking of another man (fictional or real) and he is thinking of another woman;

    or

2)   When you spend time together sexually, you shut out the world and enjoy an intimate bond and are devoted to each other emotionally, mentally and physically?

Of course, this choice is like the old commercial for deli meat that asked, "Do you want this delicious sandwich made with our deli meat or do you want the sandwich run over by a bus?" Certainly, I want a great marriage with the purest intimacy with my husband. I want to desire only him and want his desire to be only for me. And I want this close bond throughout my marriage.

God doesn't want the run-over-by-a-bus life for us either. He designed us to be one in marriage with complete unity. He created sex to be a fulfilling part of marriage, and he gives us the inside scoop on how to have an intimate relationship. His commands about sexual purity are for our protection and benefit.

Impurity in marriage has a big price tag. Impure things like watching sexually stimulating movies (pornography) break down emotional intimacy. If you are aroused or respond emotionally and mentally to a movie -- instead of to your husband -- you are looking to someone else

73

to fulfill you. Tearing down a couple's emotional intimacy can begin a downward spiral that leads to much more sin and much less sexual fulfillment.

One extreme is seen in married couples who get involved in orgies and spouse swapping. I do not believe any couple starts off their marriage thinking they would ever get involved in such gross sexual sins. Increasing impurity leads to these kinds of sins.

What about the typical challenges that Christian couples face that are not so extreme? One common temptation regarding sexual purity is addressed in this passage:

> *The husband should fulfill his marital duty to his wife, and likewise the wife to her husband. The wife's body does not belong to her alone but also to her husband. In the same way, the husband's body does not belong to him alone but also to his wife. Do not deprive each other except by mutual consent and for a time, so that you may devote yourselves to prayer. Then come together again <u>so that Satan will not tempt you</u> because of your lack of self-control.* [Emphasis added.]

> 1 Corinthians 7:3-5

This passage gives a very important guideline to married couples: Do not withhold yourselves sexually from each other, except for an agreed upon limited time, and only then for the purpose of prayer. If you withhold yourself sexually from your husband, you need to understand how Satan will use this against you and your husband. There are several things that can happen. It can erode any intimacy you have already built. It can also create fertile ground for more impurity in both of you, and begin a downward spiral in your relationship. If you are feeling emotionally disconnected, the answer isn't less sex -- it's more.

When I say "emotionally disconnected," I am talking about the day-to-day issues in life that can create a distance between a wife and husband, such as finances, parenting, busy schedules, disagreements, etc. (I am not talking about a woman who has an unfaithful husband. Some couples face critical and complicated issues that require special counseling.) But for most Christian couples, we need to understand that it is Satan who tempts us to withhold ourselves in this way. He aims to destroy your marriage. This is one of the most critical spiritual battles a married couple will face, because it can cause so many other problems in the marriage relationship.

If you are married and don't find your sexual relationship exciting, how do you turn it around? First, you must root out impurity on every level -- physically, emotionally and mentally. You may find this challenging, especially concerning emotional and mental purity, if you have freely fantasized about being with other men. It will most likely take determination to overcome this pattern in our life. But it is worth the effort because growing in your purity will create a foundation for greater intimacy with your husband.

The idea of growing in your purity is the opposite of what the world says will build a better sexual relationship in marriage. The world says that forbidden things are how to improve your sexual relationship. I recently picked up a magazine that had an article about ten fantasies to think about to help you get in the mood for sex. The majority were indecent things that a true Christian would not even think about doing.

Embracing more of the world and pursuing less godliness is not the answer to a dull sex life with your spouse. You may be stimulated by a sexy or pornographic movie or by fantasizing about being with another man, but over time it will take a toll on your intimacy as a couple. Many couples, both Christians and non-Christians, can have an exciting sexual relationship for a short time, but marriage is "till death do us part." This is not a time to be shortsighted or faithless about God's call for us to be sexually pure in body and spirit.

There are many ways to enhance your sexual relationship that are not impure. Sometimes a couple needs more information about the physiological aspects of sex to know what heightens sexual pleasure. There are books (such as *Intended for Pleasure* by Ed Wheat) that explain these things.

God created sex to be a wonderful long-term blessing of marriage that bonds us into an amazing intimacy that he describes as becoming one. This special bond in marriage can only be built through purity.

* * *

For a single woman, sexual purity means that she is pure physically, emotionally and mentally. Being single does not mean she is free to have ungodly fantasies about a man who catches her eye. She can dream about having a husband some day, but her dreams must be righteous. Earlier we looked at the Greek word *sophrosyne* which means a constant rein on all passions and desires. This is a quality that will help keep those dreams pure before God. (More about this in the next chapter.)

There may be much more at stake than you realize. If you are single and hope to marry some day -- but you have affairs of the heart -- you may never find a man who lives up to the man you have fantasized about. Or if you marry, you may find your prince is less exciting than the one in your fantasies. This may lead to some challenges in your new marriage.

Being pure physically, mentally and emotionally when you are single will give you an opportunity to build greater intimacy if you marry someday. Or if you continue your life as a single, purity will give you peace. Peace (a quality of the Holy Spirit) is one of the blessings of purity we can enjoy whether we are married or single.

The mind of sinful man is death, but the mind controlled by the Spirit is life and peace...

Romans 8:6

So then, dear friends, since you are looking forward to this, make every effort to be found spotless, blameless and at peace with him.

2 Peter 3:14

* * *

How pure do we need to be and how much effort should I put into this? Ephesians 5:3 says that there must not be even a hint of sexual immorality or any kind of impurity. This can seem like an unreasonable and unrealistic expectation if you do not understand the dangers of impurity.

> *You were taught, with regard to your former way of life, to put off your old self, <u>which is being corrupted</u> [phtheirō] by its deceitful desires; to be made new in the attitude of your minds; and to put on the new self, created to be like God in true righteousness and holiness.* [Emphasis added.]
>
> Ephesians 4:22-24

Impurity corrupts and ruins our lives. The Greek word translated "corrupted" is *phtheirō*.

Definition: *Phtheirō* (fthi'-ro); to spoil (by any process) to ruin (especially figurative by moral influences, to deprave); corrupt (self), defile, destroy.[45]

I do not want even a hint of anything that would spoil, ruin, defile or destroy my life. We may be tempted to not take this biblical warning seriously because the consequences are not immediate. It is like when Eve ate the forbidden fruit -- she did not immediately die. We can also reason that the consequences are not that bad and not take this as a serious threat.

Just because it is a hidden danger does not mean it is not real. There are many hidden dangers in our world that we know about and act upon, such as the dangers of lead poisoning. Lead poisoning can reduce a child's IQ, slow growth, cause hearing problems and damage kidneys.[46] The symptoms are not immediately seen, but we know there is a real danger. We do not want to allow even a hint of lead poisoning in our homes. The same must be true about impurity.

* * *

As we strive for purity, we must believe that it is possible. We hear too often from people in the world (including "experts") who say that we can't change. The following scripture shows that we can.

> *Do you not know that the wicked will not inherit the kingdom of God? Do not be deceived: Neither the sexually immoral nor idolaters nor adulterers nor male prostitutes nor homosexual offenders nor thieves nor the greedy nor drunkards nor slander-*

ers nor swindlers will inherit the kingdom of God. <u>And that is</u> *<u>what some of you were</u>. But you were washed, you were sancti-* *fied, you were justified in the name of the Lord Jesus Christ and* *by the Spirit of our God.* [Emphasis added.]

1 Corinthians 6:9-11

No matter what our background, by faith we can purge the impurities out of our lives. And the more we do so, the more godliness and intimacy we will enjoy.

In Chapter 1 we looked at the Greek word *katharizō* which is translated "purify" in 2 Corinthians 7:1.

Definition: *Katharizō* (kath-ar-id´-zo); to cleanse (literal or figurative); make clean, purge, purify.[47]

Purging something out of our lives will take effort. We may have to break old habits or work through deep-seated issues. The good news is that we *can* purify ourselves. In the following chapters, we will look at how God equips us to purify our thoughts and our hearts.

Worksheet 9 - Sexual Purity

What are some common deceptions we face today in regard to impurity? What scriptures can help us see the truth about these deceptions?

Do you allow yourself to have affairs of the heart? If so, what impact does this have on your purity?

Memory Verse: Ephesians 5:3

– Chapter 10 –

Pure Thoughts

The LORD detests the thoughts of the wicked, but those of the pure are pleasing to him.

Proverbs 15:26

This verse gives a very clear picture of why we need to purify our thoughts. God is not only concerned with our actions, his feelings are stirred by what we think! According to Genesis 6:5, God was grieved and his heart filled with pain because the thoughts of men were only evil.

There are many scriptures that teach us how to direct our minds. The following verses show the importance of turning our minds in a new direction and prove to us it is possible:

Love the Lord your God with all your heart and with all your soul and <u>with all your mind</u> and with all your strength. [Emphasis added.]

Mark 12:30

Those who live according to the sinful nature <u>have their minds set on</u> what that nature desires; but those who live in accordance with the Spirit <u>have their minds set on</u> what the Spirit desires. [Emphasis added.]

Romans 8:5

You were taught, with regard to your former way of life, to put off your old self, which is being corrupted by its deceitful de-

sires; <u>to be made new in the attitude of your minds</u>... [Emphasis added.]

Ephesians 4:22-23

Set your minds on things above, not on earthly things.

Colossians 3:2

Therefore, <u>prepare your minds for action</u>; be self-controlled; set your hope fully on the grace to be given you when Jesus Christ is revealed. [Emphasis added.]

1 Peter 1:13

As Christians, we can no longer just let our minds wander to whatever we want. We must set our minds on things above and prepare our minds for action. Here is why our thoughts are so important:

For <u>as he thinks within himself, so he is</u>. He says to you, "Eat and drink!" But his heart is not with you. [Emphasis added.]

Proverbs 23:7 (NASB)

Your thoughts are the real you. I find this a little frightening, because sometimes I do things out of duty -- I will say the right thing, but I'm not there in my heart. And if my thoughts were exposed, I would have some explaining to do!

* * *

In the previous chapter, we looked at the impact of sexually impure thoughts. We now will look at a broader range of thoughts -- anger, rage, bitterness, greed, fear, insecurity, doubt, guilt, etc. -- any one of which can also contaminate our spirits. If not dealt with, these things have the potential to cause us to give up our faith in God, or at the very least, make us miserable.

Our main battle as a Christian takes place within us. The Apostle Paul described his spiritual battle as "waging war against the law of my mind" (Romans 7:21-25). Paul went on to say that Jesus rescued him. As Christians, we too have been rescued (Colossians 1:13), but that does not mean the spiritual battle is over. The battle continues but we now have some new powerful weapons, and these weapons are quite unique.

*The weapons we fight with are not the weapons of the world. On
the contrary, they have divine power to demolish strongholds.*
2 Corinthians 10:4

If you are going to fight a battle you must make sure you are
equipped to fight the enemy you will face, and you need to know what
weapons will be most effective. The weapons of the world are anger, insults and threats, to name a few. These things do not demolish
strongholds, instead, they build them up. But the weapons God pro-
vides for us will demolish strongholds.

What are some strongholds in your thoughts that you need to demolish? The following are some answers I've gotten to this question:

- Thoughts that my husband doesn't love me
- I worry about whether my husband will be faithful to me
- I worry about if my husband dies what will happen to me and my
  children
- Thoughts of old boyfriends from before I became a Christian
- Sexual fantasies about someone other than my husband
- Thoughts about telling someone off who has hurt my feelings
- Wishing something bad would happen to someone who has hurt
  me
- Thoughts about cutting or hurting myself
- Thoughts about killing myself
- Dark thoughts I don't feel comfortable sharing
- Worry about money and my future
- Anxious thoughts about how I look and what others think of me
- Thoughts of self-hatred

There are many destructive thoughts we can have. The following
scriptures give us the beginning step to overcoming these kinds of
thoughts:

*Those who live according to the sinful nature have their minds
set [phroneo] on what that nature desires; but those who live*

in accordance with the Spirit have their minds set [phroneo] on what the Spirit desires.

Romans 8:5

Set your minds [phroneo] on things above, not on earthly things.

Colossians 3:2

The Greek word translated "minds set" or "set your mind" is *phroneo*.

Definition: *Phroneo* (fron-eh´-o); to exercise the mind; by implication to be mentally disposed more or less earnestly in a certain direction; intensive to interest oneself in (with concern or obedience); set the affection on.[48]

We can actually exercise our minds to develop a new way of thinking. And this is more than just a mental process. *Phroneo* means to set your affection on it. That means you will do it from your heart, not out of duty. Setting your mind on a new way of thinking and doing it from the heart will be a powerful force in purifying your thoughts.

Here are three steps that will help us exercise our minds so we can purify our thoughts: 1) learn to recognize Satan's schemes; 2) take captive every thought; and 3) make every thought obedient to Christ. Let's consider each of these in detail.

1)   Recognize Satan's Schemes

I have forgiven in the sight of Christ for your sake, in order that Satan might not outwit us. For <u>we are not unaware of his schemes</u>. [Emphasis added.]

2 Corinthians 2:10b-11

Put on the full armor of God <u>so that you can take your stand against the devil's schemes</u>. For our struggle is not against flesh and blood, but against the rulers, against the authorities, against the powers of this dark world and against the spiritual forces of evil in the heavenly realms. [Emphasis added.]

Ephesians 6:11-12

We are at war with the spiritual forces of evil around us. This isn't a physical battle that you can see, this is a battle within us. It is vital we understand how Satan tempts us so that we can fight him more ef-

83

fectively. There are two avenues that he uses. The first avenue is from inside our own hearts.

> *For out of the heart come evil thoughts...*
>
> Matthew 15:19

Our thoughts can bubble up out of our hearts -- thoughts rooted in selfishness, pride or sensuality. Satan uses past and present experiences to tempt us to be bitter or insecure, or he will use our sensual desires to tempt us to be immoral and perverse. He waits for opportune times to tempt us.

The second avenue is from outside our hearts. This is the "spiritual forces of evil in the heavenly realms." This may sound like a science fiction movie, but this is the real deal. These forces are real and we face them around the clock.

They press on us through the worldliness around us. It may be a song, an advertisement or a popular TV show. Our enemies, and even friends, can stir up an evil thought. Or perhaps it is a thought from out of the blue that's so strange or evil that you wonder why you had such a thought. If you do not recognize Satan when he lays an evil thought at the door of your heart, you can easily lose these battles. And if we allow worldly thoughts to stay in our minds, and dwell on them long enough, they will become our own.

Do you recognize the schemes Satan is using against you? Consider how Jesus fought Satan's schemes.

> *Then Jesus was led by the Spirit into the desert to be tempted by the devil. After fasting forty days and forty nights, he was hungry. The tempter came to him and said, "If you are the Son of God, tell these stones to become bread."*
>
> *Jesus answered, "It is written: 'Man does not live on bread alone, but on every word that comes from the mouth of God.'"*
>
> *Then the devil took him to the holy city and had him stand on the highest point of the temple. "If you are the Son of God," he said, "throw yourself down. For it is written:*
>
> *"'He will command his angels concerning you, and they will lift you up in their hands, so that you will not strike your foot against a stone.'"*

Jesus answered him, "It is also written: 'Do not put the Lord your God to the test.'"

Again, the devil took him to a very high mountain and showed him all the kingdoms of the world and their splendor. "All this I will give you," he said, "if you will bow down and worship me."

Jesus said to him, "Away from me, Satan! For it is written: 'Worship the Lord your God, and serve him only.'"

Then the devil left him, and angels came and attended him.
                                                                      Matthew 4:1-11

Do you think Satan came to Jesus in a physical form? I don't, because the Bible says our struggle is not against flesh and blood. I picture Jesus in a weakened state from going 40 days without food. He sees a stone that looks like a loaf of bread and he thinks, *"If you are the Son of God, tell these stones to become bread."* Jesus recognized that he was in a battle with Satan and answered him with scripture.

Then Satan tempted Jesus to throw himself off the highest point of the temple. Jesus again answered him with scripture. Finally, with complete boldness, Satan did his best to get Jesus to bow down and worship him. Jesus again quoted scripture and told Satan to go away. Then the angels came and attended Jesus.

Physically, this would have been difficult to do. Could Jesus have walked up a very high mountain after fasting 40 days? Luke 4:5 tells us that the devil showed him all the kingdoms of the world in an instant.

We don't know if Satan appeared to Jesus in a physical form, but we do know that Satan does not pop up to us that way. If he did -- like the little devil in cartoons -- our battle would be much easier. "Hey, Satan, get out of my way!" Instead, Satan sneaks up on us in our thoughts.

We can experience the same kinds of temptations that Jesus did. We can struggle at times with whether we really are a child of God. We can also be tempted to test God when our faith has grown weak. And we can be tempted to water down our Christian convictions in order to make more money. Satan can tempt us in the middle of the night when we are completely alone. He doesn't have to show up in a physical form to tempt us, but we can know for sure that he is the one we are battling!

Let's consider another encounter Jesus had with Satan, but this time Satan tries to get at Jesus through his friend Peter:

> *From that time on Jesus began to explain to his disciples that he must go to Jerusalem and suffer many things at the hands of the elders, chief priests and teachers of the law, and that he must be killed and on the third day be raised to life.*
>
> *Peter took him aside and began to rebuke him. "Never, Lord!" he said. "This shall never happen to you!"*
>
> *Jesus turned and said to Peter, "Get behind me, Satan! You are a stumbling block to me; you do not have in mind [phroneo] the things of God, but the things of men."*

Matthew 16:21-23

Satan made this temptation sound like good advice. "Jesus, you don't have to die." But Jesus again recognized Satan's scheme. Jesus told Peter that what he had his mind set on was not from God. I doubt Peter had any idea that Satan was using him to tempt Jesus, but Jesus boldly called out Satan. Jesus tested the spirits (1 John 4:1) and recognized Satan's ploys.

Whether it is the thoughts of our hearts or the forces of evil that surround us each day, we must recognize Satan's schemes. Satan has a tailor-made scheme for each one of us. His schemes are not always obvious and oftentimes appear to be comforting. He can make a temptation look appealing and even righteous, and he will defeat us if we do not recognize his scheme.

The following scripture explains how temptations lead to sin:

> *When tempted, no one should say, "God is tempting me." For God cannot be tempted by evil, nor does he tempt anyone; but each one is tempted when, by his own evil desire, he is dragged away and enticed. Then, after desire has conceived, it gives birth to sin; and sin, when it is full-grown, gives birth to death.*
> James 1:13-15

First, we are tempted. Next, we must decide if we are going to give in to this temptation. If you say yes to the temptation, you begin to sin. Finally, sin that is not dealt with will lead you to spiritual death.

The good news is that we have a choice. We can be dragged away and enticed by our desire *or* we can follow Jesus' example and say no. Temptation itself is not sin. We know that Jesus was tempted but he never sinned.

> *For we do not have a high priest who is unable to sympathize*
> *with our weaknesses, but we have one who has been tempted*
> *in every way, just as we are--yet was without sin. Let us then*
> *approach the throne of grace with confidence, so that we may*
> *receive mercy and find grace to help us in our time of need.*
>
> Hebrews 4:15-16

Promise:
You can ask for mercy
with confidence.

Jesus was tempted in every way just like us. He knows all about our struggles to be pure, and he sympathizes with us. Isn't that comforting?! And the best part of all is that Jesus never lost a battle with Satan. But that is not true of us -- we have lost plenty of them. Thankfully, we can receive God's mercy when we need it.

Are you able to ask God for mercy with confidence when you need it? Or does Satan tell you that this is impossible? This is another scheme we must recognize from Satan, because God says we can ask confidently.

Recognize

God's mercy is empowering. It helps us to get back up and continue to fight. And we will win more and more of the battles as we learn to recognize Satan's schemes. So let's approach God's throne with confidence when we need his mercy. Then let's get back into the fight for purity.

* * *

2) Take Every Thought Captive

> *We demolish arguments and every pretension that sets itself*
> *up against the knowledge of God, and we take captive every*
> *thought to make it obedient to Christ.*
>
> 2 Corinthians 10:5

The second step to exercising our minds in a new direction is to take every thought captive. In a war, if you take someone captive, you have control over them. You decide how much freedom your captives get. They can be locked up and not given any freedom, or you may allow them certain privileges.

The same is true of our thoughts. You have a choice -- you can decide how much freedom you will give a thought. You may decide to give it no freedom or, in certain circumstances, you may allow a thought to dwell in your mind even though you know you should not. Perhaps it's when you have been hurt by someone or when you have spent time with someone who influences your thinking. It's important to realize that you have a choice. You don't have to continue thinking about something.

When I first began to understand this as a young Christian, I was thrilled to think I could have control over my thoughts. This was a new concept to me. I could take a destructive, tempting, or negative thought and make it a "prisoner of war" and give it no freedom.

| Decide |

It says *every* thought, so plan to take lots of captives. Just because a thought crosses your mind does not mean you have to give it the freedom to stay. We can decide to deal with this unwanted thought.

The truth is we can have some dark thoughts. We must take them captive. As I've discussed this study with other women, they have shared some of their dark thoughts, such as jumping from a high place (remember that was Jesus' second temptation), hurting themselves, or hurting someone else. Other types of thoughts we must take captive are ungodly fantasies, critical thoughts, bitterness, anger and hatred. We also need to take captive thoughts that are centered on insecurities, doubts and fears. Recognize Satan's scheme and then decide to take these thoughts captive.

* * *

3) Make Every Thought Obedient to Christ

The third step to exercising our minds toward purity is to make our thoughts obedient to Christ. This is where we fight back. Consider the following scriptures about fighting back:

Fight the good fight of the faith...

1 Timothy 6:12

I have fought the good fight, I have finished the race, I have kept the faith.

2 Timothy 4:7-8

The weapons we fight with are not the weapons of the world. On the contrary, they have divine power to demolish strongholds.

2 Corinthians 10:4

Fight

Of course, making a thought obedient to Christ is not going to be easy. Satan is not going to walk away without a fight. And our own passions and desires do not make it easy.

"Watch and pray so that you will not fall into temptation. The spirit is willing, but the body is weak."

Mark 14:38

My spirit wants to do what's right and to think on things that are good, but my body does not give up easily. This is where our weapons with divine power help us. Let's consider some important weapons we can use.

Prayer

Do not be anxious about anything, but in everything, by prayer and petition, with thanksgiving, <u>present your requests to God. And the peace of God</u>, which transcends all understanding, <u>will guard your hearts and your minds</u> in Christ Jesus. [Emphasis added.]

Philippians 4:6-7

Promise: The peace of God will guard your heart and mind.

Prayer has divine power and is one of our most powerful weapons. This verse says that through prayer, God will guard our hearts and our minds.

When I'm in the middle of a battle in my mind, whether it be fear, worry, insecurity, bitterness, doubt, etc., I consider what I need at that moment to help me. When I know what my request is, I present it to God in prayer. I get specific about it, too. This is not the time for a general prayer. My prayer might be, "Father, help me turn my thoughts away from this bitterness. Help me forgive deeply from my heart." Or sometimes my thoughts are so overwhelming that I first have to ask God to help me clear my mind so that I can even begin to pray. The promise in this passage is that he will guard your heart and your mind and give you peace.

I have experienced the peace this verse promises. Sometimes it has taken some intense prayer, but I am amazed at how anxiety can turn to peace following such a prayer. This is truly divine power.

Openness

> If we claim to have fellowship with him yet walk in the darkness, we lie and do not live by the truth. But if we walk in the light, as he is in the light, we have fellowship with one another, and the blood of Jesus, his Son, purifies us from all sin.
>
> If we claim to be without sin, we deceive ourselves and the truth is not in us. If we confess our sins, he is faithful and just and will forgive us our sins and purify us from all unrighteousness.
>
> 1 John 1:6-9

> Therefore confess your sins to each other and pray for each other so that you may be healed. The prayer of a righteous man is powerful and effective.
>
> James 5:16

Openness is another effective weapon. We have a lot of the same struggles, but because our thoughts can be embarrassing, it can be difficult to be open about them. The following scripture explains how common our temptations are:

> No temptation has seized you except what is common to man. And God is faithful; he will not let you be tempted beyond what you can bear. But when you are tempted, he will also provide a way out so that you can stand up under it.
>
> 1 Corinthians 10:13

Promise:
God will provide a way out.

90

Satan wants you to think you are the only one who struggles the way you do. He wants you to be alone in the dark. But the truth is that our temptations are common and, if we get open about them, we can overcome them. James 5:16 says we can be healed.

I remember the first time I confessed some of my most embarrassing sins. I first asked God to make it clear who I could talk to about this. It was difficult because I felt like a real Christian should not struggle with sin. But the truth is Christians do struggle.

> *If we claim to be without sin, we deceive ourselves and the truth is not in us.*
>
> 1 John 1:8

Do you have a discipleship partner or a close spiritual friend to whom you can confess your sins and temptations? If not, I want to encourage you to develop a closer relationship with a Christian sister. A close spiritual friend can give you helpful insight that you may not see on your own.

Openness is an effective way to fight Satan. The above scriptures about confession are regarding sin rather than temptation, but I encourage you to be open about your temptations, too. You will take away much of Satan's power in your thoughts when you are open about your temptations. Satan cannot stand in the light.

The following scripture explains the challenge of being open:

> *This is the verdict: Light has come into the world, but men loved darkness instead of light because their deeds were evil. Everyone who does evil hates the light, and will not come into the light for fear that his deeds will be exposed. But whoever lives by the truth comes into the light, so that it may be seen plainly that what he has done has been done through God.*
>
> John 3:19-21

Being open about sin can stir up our fears. Don't let your fears keep you from openness. Openness is a weapon with divine power. Keep it close to you. Satan hates the light because it will give you strength and it will be obvious that God is working (John 3:21).

Meditation

> *May the words of my mouth and the meditation of my heart be pleasing in your sight, O LORD, my Rock and my Redeemer.*
>
> Psalms 19:14

> *I have hidden your word in my heart that I might not sin against you.*
>
> Psalms 119:11

To meditate means to reflect upon, study or ponder.[49] We must keep God's word close to our hearts to help us in our battles. We can do this through daily study, memorizing scriptures and taking time to ponder them as we go about our day.

The word of God is another powerful weapon we can use when we are tempted. The following scriptures describe it as a sword:

> *Take the helmet of salvation and the sword of the Spirit, which is the word of God.*
>
> Ephesians 6:17

> *For the word of God is living and active. Sharper than any double-edged sword, it penetrates even to dividing soul and spirit, joints and marrow; it judges the thoughts and attitudes of the heart.*
>
> Hebrews 4:12

This spiritual sword is an unusual weapon, because it pierces your own heart. When Jesus was quoting scriptures, he was reminding himself what was true, and it gave him the strength to not give in to Satan's temptations. Jesus said God's word is as important as the food we eat (Matthew 4:4).

Over the years as I have faced different challenges, I've used my Bible concordance and my Bible software programs to study certain topics and find scriptures to help me fight my own battles. Sometimes I've written Bible verses on index cards and kept them close so I could consider them throughout the day. I did this to help me change my thinking. When I'm tempted to hold a grudge, I need to remind myself about God's generous mercy. The scriptures remind me why I should forgive, and they set me straight about my own need for much mercy. They also help me strengthen my faith.

I remember the first time I experienced this power. I had just heard a lesson about recognizing the spiritual battles we face in our own thoughts and how to fight back with God's word. Shortly after, I was tempted to miss a church service that I usually attended. My two young children were taking long naps, and my husband had gone ahead to a deacon's meeting. As I contemplated the challenges of getting two sleepy children up by myself, the thought, "I don't want to go to church" crossed my mind. For the first time, I realized that I was in a battle with Satan in my thoughts. So I hunted for a scripture that I could use, and Hebrews 10:24-25 came to mind. This scripture helped me remember my convictions about attending church services, and I change my attitude. I got my children up, and we went to the service.

As I sat listening to the lesson, I realized what a victory I had just had. Most likely, I would have gone to the church service anyway, but I would have been sitting there feeling guilty and feeling like a hypocrite for having had the thought about not wanting to be there. Satan would have gotten me coming and going. But I recognized his scheme, engaged him in battle and won the fight.

* * *

Prayer, openness and meditation are important and powerful weapons against the tempter. The use of these spiritual weapons will strengthen us and help us win many spiritual battles.

* * *

Besides our spiritual weapons, we also have spiritual armor to protect us (Ephesians 6:13-18). I would like to briefly address two things that protect us -- faith and fellowship.

Faith

> *Now faith is being sure of what we hope for and certain of what we do not see.*
>
> Hebrews 11:1

> *In addition to all this, take up the shield of faith, with which you can extinguish all the flaming arrows of the evil one.*
>
> Ephesians 6:16

...In his great mercy he has given us new birth into a living hope through the resurrection of Jesus Christ from the dead, and into an inheritance that can never perish, spoil or fade-- kept in heaven for you, <u>who through faith are shielded by God's power</u>... [Emphasis added.]

1 Peter 1:3-5

Through our faith, we are shielded by God's power. Again, God's divine power is available to help us in our battle. Our faith is an important ingredient for winning our spiritual battles. Faith helps us see things in a new way, and it gives us certainty. It can help us demolish strongholds.

A stronghold that I had to demolish was anger and rage. I had given up on overcoming this. I thought, "This is just how I am." I remember the first time I read *"get rid of all bitterness, rage and anger..."* (Ephesians 4:31). My eyes filled with tears. I knew it must be possible if God said to do it. I had made excuses for years. My faith was helping me begin to see this stronghold in a new way. I believed God would help me overcome it.

If you are fighting your spiritual battle without faith, you will not be successful. If you don't have faith in God as you look at these scriptures, it will be a fruitless exercise. However, if you are struggling in your faith, take heart, because faith is something we can build. We can build our faith through Bible study (Romans 10:17) and through obedience (John 7:16-17). We can also ask for more faith (Luke 17:5). God can take even the tiniest bit of faith and help it grow (Matthew 17:20). And he works in our lives to help us refine our faith which he says is more precious than gold (1 Peter 1:6-7).

Fellowship

But encourage one another daily, as long as it is called Today, so that none of you may be hardened by sin's deceitfulness.

Hebrews 3:13

And let us consider how we may spur one another on toward love and good deeds. Let us not give up meeting together, as some are in the habit of doing, but let us encourage one another--and all the more as you see the Day approaching.

Hebrews 10:24-25

Fellowship is another way that God protects us. He has put us in a spiritual family to be built up and encouraged. The encouragement we get from fellowship can be a powerful shield in our lives. It can help strengthen our faith and soften our hearts. Fellow Christians are actually part of our glorious inheritance.

> *I pray also that the eyes of your heart may be enlightened in order that you may know the hope to which he has called you, the riches of his <u>glorious inheritance in his people</u>, and his incomparably great power for us who believe.* [Emphasis added.]
>
> Ephesians 1:18-19 (TNIV)

This verse does not say "glorious inheritance in heaven." It says, "glorious inheritance in his people." We know from other verses that we will have a glorious inheritance in heaven, but this verse says there is something glorious about our relationships with God's people. We don't have to wait until heaven to enjoy some of our glorious inheritance. We have each other.

If you don't see the glorious inheritance you have in God's people, Ephesians 1:18 says that you need to open your spiritual eyes. If we don't see this clearly, we can begin to miss church events or not make getting with other Christians a priority in our lives. These are symptoms of not having our spiritual eyes open.

Opening our spiritual eyes will also help us see how harmful unresolved conflicts are. We must recognize Satan's scheme in this and make every effort to work though these conflicts (Ephesians 4:3). Our Christian fellowship is to build us up and help us fight Satan. He plans to divide and destroy our Christian fellowship because he knows how much it can strengthen us.

The encouragement we receive from each other is a wonderful blessing. However, in our battle to have pure thoughts, I want to stress that there is a balance of taking responsibility and getting help from others. **Purifying your thoughts is a battle that is mostly yours to fight.** You can get all kinds of encouragement and advice from other Christians, but you have to decide to make your thoughts obedient to Christ. No one else can think for you.

* * *

Following are some examples of thoughts that we need to recognize as Satan's schemes. I encourage you to take the time to consider your thoughts and see ways you can set your mind on pure thoughts.

* * *

Doubts: Satan has a scheme for each one of us to give up our Christian life. He will use fears, doubts and anything else he can to achieve this.

Thought: *You can't do this anymore. Give up.*

Meditation: What does the Bible say?

> ..."No eye has seen, no ear has heard, no mind has conceived what God has prepared for those who love him..."
>
> 1 Corinthians 2:9

> I can do everything through him who gives me strength.
>
> Philippians 4:13

Request to God: God, help me get rid of this doubt? Please give me strength.

* * *

Marriage: If you are married, what is Satan's scheme in your marriage? Does he tempt you to be indifferent? Does he tempt you to give up? What thoughts do you need to take captive regarding your marriage?

Thought: *This marriage is not working. Walk out!*

If you are single, what is Satan's scheme for you in regard to your "singleness"? Are you content? Does he tempt you with impurity or immorality? What thoughts do you need to take captive?

Thought: _____

Meditation: What does the Bible say?

> Therefore what God has joined together, let man not separate.
>
> Mark 10:9

> Let us not become weary in doing good, for at the proper time we will reap a harvest if we do not give up.
>
> Galatians 6:9

...I have learned to be content whatever the circumstances.
Philippians 4:11

Request to God: If married: God, please help me stop thinking about ending my marriage. Help me to develop a great marriage. If single: Help me be content with my life. If single and you would like to marry some day: Help me find a godly husband.

* * *

Greed: Greed is something that can contaminate our spirits. It can create a deep dissatisfaction in us even when we are very blessed. Greed is defined as an excessive desire for getting or having more.[50] Do you struggle with thoughts prompted by greed? If so, you fill in the blank on this one.

Thought: _____

Meditation: What does the Bible say?

> *But godliness with contentment is great gain. For we brought nothing into the world, and we can take nothing out of it.*
> 1 Timothy 6:6-8

Request to God: Help me be content with what I have.

* * *

Sexually Impure thoughts: There are many sexually impure thoughts with which we can struggle. How does Satan tempt you?

Thought: _____

Meditation: What does the Bible say about it?

> *But among you there must not be even a hint of sexual immorality, or of any kind of impurity, or of greed, because these are improper for God's holy people.*
> Ephesians 5:3

> *For of this you can be sure: No immoral, impure or greedy person--such a man is an idolater--has any inheritance in the kingdom of Christ and of God*
> Ephesians 5:5

Request to God: God, help me be pure in my thoughts.

* * *

Bitterness: Bitterness is something that develops because of past hurts. It may be a family member or an old boyfriend or something your spouse did. Does Satan tempt you with bitterness or a lack of forgiveness?

Thought: _____

Meditation: What does the Bible say about it?

> *The godless in heart harbor resentment...*
>
> Job 36:13

> *Get rid of all bitterness, rage and anger, brawling and slander, along with every form of malice. Be kind and compassionate to one another, forgiving each other, just as in Christ God forgave you.*
>
> Ephesians 4:31-32

Request to God: God help me forgive this old hurt from my heart. Help me remember how much forgiveness you have given me.

* * *

Take time to consider your thoughts, confess them, find scriptures that strengthen you, and spend time in prayer. I don't want to give the impression that this is an easy 1-2-3, because it isn't. It is a spiritual battle that we each must fight. Let's be faithful and determined to purify our thoughts.

Worksheet 10 - Pure Thoughts

What are Satan's schemes in your thoughts?

_____

_____

_____

What thoughts do you need to purify?

_____

_____

_____

Are you open about your temptations and sins?

Consider what you think about during the day. Ask God to help you identify thoughts that are harmful to you.

_____

_____

_____

_____

_____

_____

_____

_____

_____

_____

_____

_____

Memory Verse: Romans 12:2

– Chapter 11 –

Pure Words

If anyone considers himself religious and yet does not keep a tight rein on his tongue, he deceives himself and his religion is worthless.

James 1:26

Speech is another area of our lives that we must purify. Our religion is actually worthless if we don't watch what we say. Whether we are young Christians or older Christians, our speech is something we continually need to purify.

For new Christians, it may be that they need to turn from lies or coarse joking. For those who have been Christians for years, it may be that their challenges are less obvious. Perhaps their struggle is with bitter words, critical words or words driven by pride. Following are several areas of speech that the Bible addresses:

Slander

The following verses specifically address women:

Likewise, teach the older women to be reverent in the way they live, not to be slanderers [diabolos] or addicted to much wine, but to teach what is good.

Titus 2:3

In the same way, their wives are to be women worthy of respect, not malicious talkers [diabolos] but temperate and trustworthy in everything.

1 Timothy 3:11

Definition: *Diabolos* (dee-ab´-ol-os); a traducer; especially Satan; false accuser, devil, slanderer.[51]

The word traducer means someone who says untrue or malicious things about someone; one who defames, slanders or vilifies. Slander means the utterance in the presence of another person of a false statement or statements that are damaging to a third person's character or reputation.[52]

The Greek word *diabolos* is translated "Satan" 34 times in the Bible.[53] Satan is our accuser (Revelation 12:10). This is the opposite of God. Consider the following verse:

> *...the God who gives life to the dead and calls things that are not as though they were.*
>
> Romans 4:17

God called Gideon a mighty warrior, and Jesus called Peter a rock. Both of these men lived up to their new names. There are many other examples in the Bible of people who were changed in a great way by their relationship with God.

We can be like Satan or we can be like God. The words we use can have a powerful effect on those around us.

> *The tongue has the power of life and death, and those who love it will eat its fruit.*
>
> Proverbs 18:21

Just as positive words can call people higher, negative words can discourage or destroy. How easy it is to say something negative or to voice an opinion that brings someone into a bad light. And how unlike God I am when I speak ill about someone. Slander has serious consequences.

> *LORD, who may dwell in your sanctuary? Who may live on your holy hill? He whose walk is blameless and who does what is righteous, who speaks the truth from his heart and has no slander on his tongue, who does his neighbor no wrong and casts no slur on his fellowman...*
>
> Psalms 15:1-3

But now I am writing you that you must not associate with anyone who calls himself a brother but is sexually immoral or greedy, an idolater or a slanderer, a drunkard or a swindler. With such a man do not even eat.

1 Corinthians 5:11

Brothers, do not slander one another. Anyone who speaks against his brother or judges him speaks against the law and judges it. When you judge the law, you are not keeping it, but sitting in judgment on it.

James 4:11

Gossip

Gossip can be appealing because it is a way for us to get connected with others. It can give us a sense of belonging in the neighborhood or in the workplace. Even if we believe it is wrong and decide we should not do it, we can find ourselves engaged in a conversation full of gossip. Not wanting to participate, yet not wanting to be excluded is certainly a difficult position. If you choose not to gossip, you may not only be excluded but also the focus of the gossip.

Gossip is a pet sin of the world. There are many magazines and television shows that are founded on gossip. Gossip is clearly an example of the choice we have of being a friend of the world or a friend of God (James 4:4). We need to understand how harmful gossip is.

A gossip betrays a confidence; so avoid a man who talks too much.

Proverbs 20:19

A perverse man stirs up dissension, and a gossip separates close friends.

Proverbs 16:28

The words of a gossip are like choice morsels; they go down to a man's inmost parts.

Proverbs 26:22

Your innermost part is your heart. Something that seems as small as a little gossip can corrupt your heart. It can turn you against someone and destroy a relationship that had previously been very close.

Complaining/Arguing

> *Do everything without complaining or arguing, so that you may become blameless and pure...*
>
> Philippians 2:14-15

Complaining or arguing can also keep us from being pure. It also says we will not be blameless if we argue and complain. Consider what Jesus says about our words in the following passage:

> *"But I tell you that men will have to give account on the day of judgment for every careless word they have spoken. For by your words you will be acquitted, and by your words you will be condemned."*
>
> Matthew 12:36-37

Complaints and arguments can be a burden to those around us, and these kinds of words can keep us from the purity we are pursuing.

* * *

There are many kinds of impure words that create problems in our relationships with each other and with God. Following are some more words we are called to purify:

Lying/Deceit

> *Reckless words pierce like a sword, but the tongue of the wise brings healing. Truthful lips endure forever, but a lying tongue lasts only a moment.*
>
> Proverbs 12:18-19

> *The tongue that brings healing is a tree of life, but a deceitful tongue crushes the spirit.*
>
> Proverbs 15:4

Course Joking/Foolish Talk

> *But among you there must not be even a hint of sexual immorality, or of any kind of impurity, or of greed, because these are improper for God's holy people. <u>Nor should there be obscenity, foolish talk or coarse joking, which are out of place, but rather thanksgiving</u>.* [Emphasis added.]
>
> Ephesians 5:3-4

103

Anger/Rage

A fool gives full vent to his anger, but a wise man keeps himself under control.

Proverbs 29:11

Get rid of all bitterness, rage and anger, brawling and slander, along with every form of malice.

Ephesians 4:31

Filthy Language

But now you must rid yourselves of all such things as these: anger, rage, malice, slander, and filthy language from your lips.

Colossians 3:8

Swearing

Above all, my brothers, do not swear--not by heaven or by earth or by anything else. Let your "Yes" be yes, and your "No," no, or you will be condemned.

James 5:12

Cursing

Bless those who persecute you; bless and do not curse.

Romans 12:14

If a man curses his father or mother, his lamp will be snuffed out in pitch darkness.

Proverbs 20:20

Too Many Words

The more the words, the less the meaning, and how does that profit anyone?

Ecclesiastes 6:11

When words are many, sin is not absent, but he who holds his tongue is wise.

Proverbs 10:19

* * *

The following passage explains the battle we face with our speech:

Likewise the tongue is a small part of the body, but it makes great boasts. Consider what a great forest is set on fire by a small spark. The tongue also is a fire, a world of evil among the parts of the body. It corrupts the whole person, sets the whole course of his life on fire, and is itself set on fire by hell.

All kinds of animals, birds, reptiles and creatures of the sea are being tamed and have been tamed by man, but no man can tame the tongue. It is a restless evil, full of deadly poison.

With the tongue we praise our Lord and Father, and with it we curse men, who have been made in God's likeness. Out of the same mouth come praise and cursing. My brothers, this should not be.

James 3:5-12

This scripture gives us a clear picture of the impact of our words. Just like a spark in a forest, our words can start a sequence of events that we cannot control.

We are told we cannot tame the tongue. So you may be wondering why then are we discussing this if it is out of our control. Jesus explains this in the following verse:

The good man brings good things out of the good stored up in his heart, and the evil man brings evil things out of the evil stored up in his heart. For out of the overflow of his heart his mouth speaks.

Luke 6:45

The words you speak actually flow out of your heart. You cannot tame the tongue; it is going to reveal what is in your heart. This does not mean you have no solution though. Your solution is to work on your heart when you need to change something about your speech. If something comes out of your mouth that should not, you need to consider what is going on in your heart. If you work only on the external, you will not be very successful because your tongue is going to reveal your heart.

What is in a person's heart who speaks angry, hurtful words? Perhaps it is pride or hatred. Why does someone slander another person? Again, maybe it is pride, hatred or insecurity. What is behind gossip? Perhaps it is people-pleasing or trying to gain power or influence with someone. We need to consider our hearts when it comes to the words we use and consider what is going on in our hearts.

It is tempting to blame someone else. It is easy to think, "If they had not made me angry, I would not have said it." But we have a choice. It is important to see Satan's schemes and how we respond to them. We need to recognize, decide and fight. Fight Satan -- not the person with whom you are upset.

* * *

God tells us that we can actually change our hearts:

> Rid yourselves of all the offenses you have committed, and get a new heart and a new spirit. Why will you die, O house of Israel?
>
> Ezekiel 18:31

> I will give you a new heart and put a new spirit in you; I will remove from you your heart of stone and give you a heart of flesh.
>
> Ezekiel 36:26

> Those whom I love I rebuke and discipline. So be earnest, and repent.
>
> Revelation 3:19

God calls us to be earnest and repent when we see a need to make changes. He even offers to give us a new heart. How amazing that is! God helps us in every way. Our part is to humbly turn to him. It may take special days of fasting and prayer, but God wants to help us change our hearts. The new heart he wants us to have is one of love. Love sums up all the laws of the Bible:

> The entire law is summed up in a single command: "Love your neighbor as yourself." If you keep on biting and devouring each other, watch out or you will be destroyed by each other.
>
> Galatians 5:14-15

* * *

We are also given direction in the scriptures on what kinds of words are loving and helpful. Following are a few of them:

> Do not let any unwholesome talk come out of your mouths, but only what is helpful for building others up according to their needs, that it may benefit those who listen.
>
> Ephesians 4:29

A gentle answer turns away wrath, but a harsh word stirs up anger.

Proverbs 15:1

Do not repay evil with evil or insult with insult, but with blessing, because to this you were called so that you may inherit a blessing. For, "Whoever would love life and see good days must keep his tongue from evil and his lips from deceitful speech."

1 Peter 3:9-10

Pleasant words are a honeycomb, sweet to the soul and healing to the bones.

Proverbs 16:24

Instead, speaking the truth in love, we will in all things grow up into him who is the Head, that is, Christ.

Ephesians 4:15

Therefore encourage one another and build each other up, just as in fact you are doing.

1 Thessalonians 5:11

...give thanks in all circumstances, for this is God's will for you in Christ Jesus.

1 Thessalonians 5:18

Through Jesus, therefore, let us continually offer to God a sacrifice of praise--the fruit of lips that confess his name.

Hebrews 13:15

Our words are powerful. They can heal or destroy. It is no wonder that there are so many scriptures in the Bible devoted to our speech. If you are challenged in a specific area of speech, take the time to consider what the Bible has to say about it and what is going on in your heart. To be a true Christian, you must keep a tight rein on your tongue (James 1:26).

May the words of my mouth and the meditation of my heart be pleasing in your sight, O LORD, my Rock and my Redeemer.

Psalms 19:14

Worksheet 11 - Pure Words

Consider each area of speech from the previous pages. In which of these areas do you struggle to control your words? (Slander, gossip, complaining, arguing, lying, deceit, course joking, foolish talk, anger, rage, filthy language, swearing, cursing, etc.)

_____

_____

_____

What is in your heart that causes these words to come out of your mouth? In other words, what do you need to focus on to change this?

_____

_____

_____

_____

_____

Are you known for building others up through your words?

Do you use gentle words in response to harsh words?

Do you guard your mouth (Proverbs 21:23)?

Consider again the scriptures describing the kinds of words we should speak. Which of these are your strengths? Which of these would you like to improve?

_____

_____

_____

_____

Memory Verse: Psalms 19:14

– Chapter 12 –

A Pure Heart

Blessed are the pure in heart, for they will see God.
                                        Matthew 5:8

Promise:
You will see God.

We began this study about purity by looking at 2 Corinthians 6:16-18 where God tells us that he wants to be a Father to us, walk with us and live with us. We will conclude this study with the promise that the pure in heart will be blessed -- they will see God! What an amazing promise. If we have a pure heart, we will see the Lord Almighty! With this promise in mind, consider the following verse:

Above all else, guard your heart, for it is the wellspring of life.
                                        Proverbs 4:23

A wellspring is the source of a stream or underground well. Your heart is like a wellspring -- it is what fills up your life.

The good man brings good things out of the good stored up in his heart, and the evil man brings evil things out of the evil stored up in his heart. <u>For out of the overflow of his heart</u> his mouth speaks. [Emphasis added.]
                                        Luke 6:45

Your heart overflows into all the areas of your life, whether it is your choice of clothing or entertainment, your thoughts or words, or how interested you are in spiritual beauty. Your heart is revealed by your choices.

Purifying our hearts is a lifetime pursuit. Sarah and Naomi are examples of older women who were still coming to grips with impure attitudes flowing from their hearts. Sarah scoffed at the thought of having a baby in her old age, but she learned that nothing was too hard for the Lord (Genesis 18:12-14). Naomi struggled with bitter disappointment, but found that God had not stopped showing her kindness (Ruth 1:20; 2:20). They both held on to their faith and fought their battles for a pure heart.

We must do the same thing. No matter how old we are or how long we have been a Christian, we must continue to purify our hearts. This is our wellspring that fills up our lives. Let's guard it carefully.

Following are four spiritual heart conditions that we need to consider:

A Deceitful Heart

> *The heart is deceitful above all things and beyond cure. Who can understand it?*
>
> Jeremiah 17:9

We can believe something deep down in our hearts and be wrong! The first example of a deceived heart is when Eve believed Satan's lie (Genesis 3:4). Her deceived heart told her not to trust God, so she took things into her own hands and disobeyed God. Unfortunately, like Eve, we can also be deceived.

> *But I am afraid that just as Eve was deceived by the serpent's cunning, your minds may somehow be led astray from your sincere and pure devotion to Christ.*
>
> 2 Corinthians 11:3

Satan tries to deceive us in many ways. He is a liar and a deceiver.

> *You belong to your father, the devil, and you want to carry out your father's desire. He was a murderer from the beginning, not holding to the truth, for there is no truth in him. When he lies, he speaks his native language, for he is a liar and the father of lies.*
>
> John 8:44

The great dragon was hurled down--that ancient serpent called the devil, or Satan, <u>who leads the whole world astray</u>. He was hurled to the earth, and his angels with him. [Emphasis added.]

Revelation 12:9

Satan is always working to deceive us, and he is good at it. He can make something dangerous look appealing, or something that is perverse look fun. He is the father of lies, and he speaks them to us every day.

There are several ways that we can protect ourselves from deception. One is by daily contact with other Christians. When we stay close to each other, it is much harder for Satan to deceive us.

But encourage one another daily, as long as it is called Today, so that none of you may be hardened by sin's deceitfulness.

Hebrews 3:13

Another way is by studying God's word. God's word will help us discern the thoughts and attitudes of our hearts and see spiritual truths more clearly (Hebrews 4:12). In addition to studying it, we also need to love it. Loving the truth and obeying God's word will protect our hearts.

The coming of the lawless one will be in accordance with the work of Satan displayed in all kinds of counterfeit miracles, signs and wonders, and in every sort of evil that deceives those who are perishing. <u>They perish because they refused to love the truth</u> and so be saved. [Emphasis added.]

2 Thessalonians 2:9-10

To the Jews who had believed him, Jesus said, "If you hold to my teaching, you are really my disciples. Then you will know the truth, and the truth will set you free."

John 8:31-32

> Promises:
> You will know the truth.
> You will be set free.

Loving the truth is not always easy, because the truth can sometimes hurt. But not loving the truth will cost us everything.

* * *

A Secretive Heart

If we had forgotten the name of our God or spread out our hands to a foreign god, would not God have discovered it, since he knows the secrets of the heart?

Psalms 44:20-21

For God will bring every deed into judgment, including every hidden thing, whether it is good or evil.

Ecclesiastes 12:14

God is always searching our hearts (Jeremiah 17:10), and he knows all our secrets. I like to think of this as his protection. He knows hidden sin will destroy us.

"Woe to you, teachers of the law and Pharisees, you hypocrites! You are like whitewashed tombs, which look beautiful on the outside but on the inside are full of dead men's bones and everything unclean."

Matthew 23:27

A whitewashed tomb is a good picture of hidden sin -- pretty on the outside, but entirely unclean on the inside. Some sins we can hide in our hearts are pride, lust, hatred, malice, envy, jealousy, anger, greed, idolatry, selfish ambition and deceit.

To overcome this heart condition, we have to be open and humble. Coming into the light (confessing sin) is the solution for a secretive heart. This is how we live by the truth.

"This is the verdict: Light has come into the world, but men loved darkness instead of light because their deeds were evil. Everyone who does evil hates the light, and will not come into the light for fear that his deeds will be exposed. But whoever lives by the truth comes into the light, so that it may be seen plainly that what he has done has been done through God." [Emphasis added.]

John 3:19-21

Note: There are secrets that we can and should keep. Jesus explains in the following verse:

"Be careful not to do your 'acts of righteousness' before men, to be seen by them. If you do, you will have no reward from your Father in heaven. So when you give to the needy, do not an-

112

nounce it with trumpets, as the hypocrites do in the synagogues and on the streets, to be honored by men. I tell you the truth, they have received their reward in full. But when you give to the needy, do not let your left hand know what your right hand is doing, so that your giving may be in secret. Then your Father, who sees what is done in secret, will reward you."

Matthew 6:1-4

Promise:
You will be rewarded.

The only secret we should keep is the good we do, but we need to be completely open about the sins in our hearts. Isn't this the opposite of our sinful nature? I would much rather talk about the good I do rather than the bad. But doing it God's way will help us stay humble and protect our hearts.

* * *

An Unbelieving Heart

See to it, brothers, that none of you has a sinful, unbelieving heart that turns away from the living God.

Hebrews 3:12

And without faith it is impossible to please God, because anyone who comes to him must believe that he exists and that he rewards those who earnestly seek him.

Hebrews 11:6

We typically think of an unbeliever as a non-Christian; however, these scriptures address Christians. Remaining faithful is one of our greatest challenges. We can have a strong faith for a long time, but then suddenly find ourselves struggling. We may not even know how it happened. Symptoms include not praying, not studying the scriptures, not obeying the scriptures and not being open about sin.

We can go through the motions of being religious. We can show up at a church service, smile and greet people, but then go home and struggle with serious sins. It is our faith that helps us open up about our sin. It is our faith that helps us turn to God in prayer about our heartaches and disappointments, and it's our faith that helps us turn from worldliness.

Even strong Christians can have areas of unbelief that they must work through. Elijah is an example of this. He displayed great faith when he challenged the 450 prophets of Baal, but ran away when the queen threatened his life. God helped him find strength and he overcame his faithlessness (1 Kings 18-19). We must take any area of faithlessness in our lives very seriously, because it can get to the point that our faith is destroyed.

> *Timothy, my son, I give you this instruction in keeping with the prophecies once made about you, so that by following them you may fight the good fight, holding on to faith and a good conscience. Some have rejected these and so have shipwrecked their faith.*
>
> 1 Timothy 1:18-19

Our faith is tested in many ways. We must remember that this is a good thing. Our faith is more precious than gold (1 Peter 1:7). When God refines us through trials, he is helping us gain something of great value. Abraham is an example of someone whose faith grew as he went through his trials.

> *Against all hope, Abraham in hope believed and so became the father of many nations, just as it had been said to him, "So shall your offspring be." Without weakening in his faith, he faced the fact that his body was as good as dead--since he was about a hundred years old--and that Sarah's womb was also dead. Yet he did not waver through unbelief regarding the promise of God, but was strengthened in his faith and gave glory to God, being fully persuaded that God had power to do what he had promised.* [Emphasis added.]
>
> Romans 4:18-21

Satan has many schemes to weaken our faith. They include challenging times as well as times when we are blessed. I have seen Christians persevere through some of the most challenging trials, then later walk away from God when they were blessed with material things. Our goal must be to grow in our faith more and more, because we do not know what challenges lie ahead.

We ought always to thank God for you, brothers, and rightly so, because your faith is growing more and more, and the love every one of you has for each other is increasing.

2 Thessalonians 1:3

A Hard Heart

They are darkened in their understanding and separated from the life of God because of the ignorance that is in them due to the hardening of their hearts. Having lost all sensitivity, they have given themselves over to sensuality so as to indulge in every kind of impurity, with a continual lust for more.

Ephesians 4:18-19

Our hearts harden when we sin. This is true for both Christians and non-Christians. The result of a hard heart is spiritual ignorance and the loss of our sensitivity to what is right and wrong. Another symptom is that we cannot see or hear spiritual truths.

For this people's heart has become calloused; they hardly hear with their ears, and they have closed their eyes. Otherwise they might see with their eyes, hear with their ears, understand with their hearts and turn, and I would heal them.

Acts 28:27

Our hearts can harden because of the deceitfulness of sin or because of bitter disappointments. One specific sin that hardens our hearts is pride. The following verse describes what happened to the powerful King Nebuchadnezzar:

But when his heart became arrogant and hardened with pride, he was deposed from his royal throne and stripped of his glory.

Daniel 5:20

Success and power will test our hearts. Even spiritual accomplishments can test us. In the following passage, Jesus contrasts a prideful prayer and a humble prayer.

To some who were confident of their own righteousness and looked down on everybody else, Jesus told this parable: "Two men went up to the temple to pray, one a Pharisee and the other a tax collector. The Pharisee stood up and prayed about himself: 'God, I thank you that I am not like other men--robbers, evildoers, adulterers--or even like this tax collector. I fast twice a week and give a tenth of all I get.'"

115

> *"But the tax collector stood at a distance. He would not even look up to heaven, but beat his breast and said, 'God, have mercy on me, a sinner.'"*
>
> *"I tell you that this man, rather than the other, went home justified before God. For everyone who exalts himself will be humbled, and he who humbles himself will be exalted."*
>
> Luke 18:9-14

Hardness of heart is the most frightening heart condition, because a hardhearted or prideful person does not see their need for God. And a hard heart does not respond to spiritual input. But there is still hope for a hardhearted person, because God can humble us. Nebuchadnezzar learned this lesson.

> *Now I, Nebuchadnezzar, praise and exalt and glorify the King of heaven, because everything he does is right and all his ways are just. <u>And those who walk in pride he is able to humble</u>.* [Emphasis added.]
>
> Daniel 4:37

God humbles us in different ways. Sometimes he humbles us through his love. Feeling God's love can be a very humbling experience. Another way he humbles us is through discipline. Nebuchadnezzar is an example of someone who was humbled by discipline.

Thankfully, God can humble a prideful heart, but a better solution is to learn to humble ourselves (James 4:10; 1 Peter 5:5-6). This is something we can learn to do. However, it will take practice -- seek advice about your life, be open about the things you are ashamed of, and pray like David did in the following scriptures:

> *Search me, O God, and know my heart; test me and know my anxious thoughts. See if there is any offensive way in me, and lead me in the way everlasting.*
>
> Psalms 139:23-24

> *Create in me a pure heart, O God, and renew a steadfast spirit within me.*
>
> Psalms 51:10

There is nothing more important than protecting your heart. Remember, it is the wellspring of your life. Guard it carefully!

* * *

PURSUING PURITY

Purity is one of our greatest protections. It insulates us from many troubles of the world. Impurity is one of our greatest threats. It hardens our hearts and distorts our view of spiritual truths. God offers us an amazing opportunity when he calls us to purify ourselves.

It's important that we remember that the purity we enjoy is really a gift from God. Only through God's word, his Holy Spirit and his amazing sacrifice for our sins can we enjoy any purity at all. And his ongoing mercy helps us get back up and keep going when we have lost a battle. Without God, we could not even begin to purify ourselves, so we should give God all the glory for the purity we are gaining in our lives.

> *It is God who arms me with strength and makes my way perfect.*
> *He makes my feet like the feet of a deer; he enables me to stand*
> *on the heights.*
>
> Psalms 18:32-33

Let's pursue purity and enjoy its protection, power and peace, and to God be the glory!

Worksheet 12 - A Pure Heart

Do you guard your heart above all else?

In what ways do you guard your heart?

When do you struggle with your faith?

Do you have areas of unbelief in your heart? If so, what are they?

What helps you build your faith?

When do you struggle with pride?

How do you fight pride in your heart?

Memory Verse: Proverbs 4:23

NOTES

1. James Strong, *Strong's Exhaustive Concordance* (Nashville, Tennessee: Crusade Bible Publishers, Inc.), [Bible Explorer 4.0].
2. "Spiritual Progress Hard to Find in 2003," (http://www.barna.org/Flex-Page.aspx?Page=BarnaUpdate&BarnaUpdateID=155/, 2003).
3. Strong.
4. Ibid.
5. Dr. Nancy Etcoff, Dr. Susie Orbach, Dr. Jennifer Scott, and Heidi D'Agostino, "The Real Truth About Beauty: A Global Report," (http://www.campaignforrealbeauty.com/uploadedfiles/dove_white_paper_final.pdf, 2004), pp. 2, 10, 11.
6. Ibid., p. 6.
7. Webster's New World Dictionary Third College Edition (New York, New York: Simon & Schuster, Inc., 1988), p. 122.
8. Etcoff, Orbach, Scott and D'Agostino, p. 3.
9. W. E. Vine, *Vine's Expository Dictionary of Old and New Testament Words* (Tarrytown, NY: Fleming H. Revell Company), [Bible Explorer 4.0].
10. Ibid.
11. Ibid.
12. Ibid.
13. Strong.
14. Virginia Lefler, *A Gentle & Quiet Spirit* (Grayslake, Illinois: Silverday Press, 2006), pp. 10-13.
15. Etcoff, Orbach, Scott and D'Agostino, p. 40.
16. Vine.
17. Lefler, pp.5-7.
18. Etcoff, Orbach, Scott and D'Agostino, p. 25.
19. John L. Jeffcoat III, "English Bible History" (http://www.greatsite.com/timeline-english-bible-history/, 2002).
20. dc talk and The Voice of the Martyrs, *Jesus Freaks* (Tulsa, Oklahoma: Albury Publishing, 1999), pp. 41-42.
21. Herbert Lockyer, *All the Women of the Bible* (Grand Rapids, Michigan: Zondervan Publishing House, 1946), p. 14.
22. Ibid.
23. Strong.
24. Webster's.
25. Ibid.
26. Vine.
27. Webster's.
28. Vine.

29. Webster's.

30. Robert Jamieson, A. R. Fausset, and David Brown, *Jamieson-Fausset-Brown Bible Commentary* (http://www.studylight.org/com/jfb/view.cgi?book=es&chapter=002).

31. Etcoff, Orbach, Scott and D'Agostino, p. 25.

32. Diane Levin, Ph.D., "So Sexy, So Soon: The Sexualization of Childhood in Commercial Culture" (http://www.commercialexploitation.com/articles/4thsummit/levin.htm).

33. Maria Mooshil, "Lizzie Shows Sexy Sizzle" *Chicago Tribune*, February 21, 2006, Sec. 5, p. 1.

34. Ibid, p. 7.

35. "The Production Code" (http://en.wikipedia.org/wiki/Hays_Code., 1930).

36. Patricia M. Jones, "TV Terror," *Chicago Tribune*, October 18, 2005, Tempo Section, p. 1.

37. Internet Filter Review (http://internet-filter-review.toptenreviews.com/internet-pornography-statistics.html) September, 2003.

38. Ibid.

39. Vine.

40. "Sexually Transmitted Diseases, General Information," Centers for Disease Control (http://www.cdc.gov/nchstp/dstd/disease_info.htm), 2004.

41. Avert Global HIV/AIDS estimates, end of 2005 (http://www.avert.org/worldstats.htm), 2005.

42. National Right to Life (http://www.nrlc.org/abortion/facts/abortionstats.html).

43. "Genital HPV Infection - CDC Fact Sheet", Centers for Disease Control (http://www.cdc.gov/std/HPV/STDFact-HPV.htm), 2004.

44. Ipsos BookTrends, Book Industry Study Group and American Bookseller Association reports (https://www.rwanational.org), 2004.

45. Strong.

46. The National Library of Medicine, Medline Plus (http://www.nlm.nih.gov/medlineplus/ency/article/002473.htm#Symptoms).

47. Strong.

48. Ibid.

49. Webster's.

50. Ibid.

51. Strong.

52. Webster's.

53. Vine.

A Gentle & Quiet Spirit - Revised Edition

By Virginia Lefler

A NEW PERSPECTIVE FOR TODAY'S CHRISTIAN WOMAN

*…the unfading beauty of a gentle and quiet spirit, which is
of great worth in God's sight.*
- 1 Peter 3:4

Many Christian women face a dilemma in embracing the biblical teaching about a gentle and quiet spirit. They want to please God but they perceive "gentle" and "quiet" as weak or passive qualities. The truth is that the original Greek text describes a strong and peaceful woman, and the word translated "great worth" means the very end or limit with reference to value. In other words, there is nothing more valuable to God. This book will give you a new perspective and some valuable lessons in how to become this strong woman with inner peace. Twenty-five worksheets throughout the book make it especially useful as a personal or group study guide.

Books and teaching aids by Virginia Lefler are available at:

SilverdayPress.com

NOTES